# GIVING UP
# IS NOT AN OPTION

# GIVING UP
# IS NOT AN OPTION

*The Purpose for the Pain*

Sharon L. Grant

DESTINY IMAGE® PUBLISHERS, INC.

P.O. Box 310, Shippensburg, PA 17257-0310

*"Speaking to the Purposes of God for This Generation and for the Generations to Come."*

This book and all other Destiny Image, Revival Press, MercyPlace, Fresh Bread, Destiny Image Fiction, and Treasure House books are available at Christian bookstores and distributors worldwide.

For a U.S. bookstore nearest you, call 1-800-722-6774.
For more information on foreign distributors, call 717-532-3040.
Reach us on the Internet: www.destinyimage.com.

ISBN 10: 0-7684-3153-0
ISBN 13: 978-0-7684-3153-7

*For Worldwide Distribution, Printed in the U.S.A.*
1 2 3 4 5 6 7 8 9 10 11 / 13 12 11 10

# In Memory of:

Rev. Terry Von-Eric Grant
Deacon Thomas and Mrs. Lula Ashford
Ms. Luevonia Thompson
Miss Kim Bolton
Dr. Joseph S. Grant Jr.
Miss Ericka J. Grant
Ms. Vikki Richardson

# ACKNOWLEDGMENTS

My sincere thanks and heartfelt love for allowing me to discover who I am without giving up on me is extended to my three daughters who are known as my T.A.G. Team (Tawanna, Alexandria, and Gabrielle). I am a proud mother and am excited that I didn't give up when I wanted to because I would have missed all that God has created them to be.

Thank you to my wonderful parents, Pastor Thomas Ashford and First Lady Barbara, who have always been an encouragement and a blessing to me. Thanks to Mr. Eugene and Mrs. Celina Cole, LeBraun Cole, Miss Wanda and Celine Ashford, and Mrs. Jean Gibbs Terry-Grant for encouraging, praying, and being there for me during the best and worst of times. I am glad to be a part of this family. To all of my family and friends, thank you for your words of wisdom, prayers, and support.

Many thanks go to my extended church family. My heartfelt gratitude to family and friends of New Jerusalem Missionary Baptist Church in East Point, Georgia. A special thanks to Bishop T.D. Jakes and First Lady Serita for unselfishly teaching and preaching the Word of God. You have made an impact on my life that will never be erased. I also wish to thank Pastor and First Lady Derick and Tanya Faison, Pastor and First Lady Rodney and Ramona Derrick, and Pastor and First Lady Timothy and

Juliette Ross for seeing something in me that I didn't see myself. Thank you for your continued prayers and words of wisdom to ensure that I kept moving forward in God's purpose. Thanks also to all the associate pastors, elders, ministers, and congregants of The Potter's House.

Thank you to all pastors, ministers, and conference coordinators who have opened their doors for me to minister to the people of God. A special thanks to Pastor John E. Butler and Pastor Samuel D. Obie for giving me the first opportunity to preach the Word of God. Though I was scared and was a bit long-winded, you encouraged me to keep going. I have been blessed beyond measure to witness all that God has done in the lives of His people.

And thanks to all of you who will read *Giving Up is Not An Option: The Purpose for the Pain*. I pray that a word of encouragement will leap from these pages and catapult you into fulfilling your God-given purpose.

# Endorsements

Please don't let the title of this book fool you! These are not the words of a motivational speaker or inspirational teacher. Beyond the cover of this book you will hear from someone who has actually lived every word written on these pages. From tragedy to triumph and every step in between, Sharon displays a level of transparency that I do not find in most writers. It is because of this I am convinced that *giving up is not an option*!

Pastor Timothy Charles Ross
Associate Pastor of The Potter's House

*Giving Up is Not An Option* is a must-read for anyone who has suffered tremendous setbacks in life. Sharon's journey through tragedy and turmoil to ultimate triumph will infuse readers with the necessary fortitude to forge ahead in life. You will walk away knowing for certain that because God will NEVER give up on you, you are destined to win!

Cheryl L. Thomas
Author & Founder of
Becoming Engaged Enterprises, Inc.
Dallas, Texas

*Giving Up is Not An Option: The Purpose for the Pain* articulates not only the anguish and sorrow but, more importantly, the assurance of the Lord's love and presence in it. Through her courage and testimony, Sharon urges us all to walk through life's "nevertheless" seasons, moment by moment. *"That I may know Him, and the power of His resurrection, and the fellowship of His sufferings"* (Phil. 3:10)—Sharon Grant not only describes the journey through the valley of the shadows but also the victories to be celebrated along the way.

Rev. Robyn L. McCoy
Founder of The Master's Touch

*Giving Up is Not An Option* sets the reader on an amazing journey of discovering how life's pain and circumstances can achieve a significant purpose for God. Sharon Grant uses the testimony of her own personal tragedy to reveal the glorious riches of the Cross and God's uncanny ability and desire to usher you into the destiny He has prepared for you. Upon finishing this book, you will know beyond a shadow of a doubt that *giving up is not an option!*

Evangelist Nichelle L. Early
Founder of PreachingWoman.com
BreakForth Ministries and Consulting

# TABLE OF CONTENTS

# FOREWORD

The human experience is one that is filled with tragedy and triumph. As a pastor, I have been blessed to rejoice with people who have enjoyed great success…but I have also stood by and prayed with those who have had great struggles and heartache. We have all had our share of both in our individual lives. At the intersection of these sometimes conflicting extremes, we are often blessed to cross paths with individuals who seem to possess a unique ability to face life with a grace and demeanor that demands admiration. Elder Sharon Grant is one of those individuals.

Sitting in my office and having my first brief meeting with this poised woman of God made me pose the question, "Who are you in God that I should know you?" As she shared the things in her life that made her into the woman of God that I have witnessed, it became clear to me that this is a gift that will soon leave an indelible mark on the Kingdom of God. The anointing for ministry seemed to ooze from the pores of her skin.

With poignant truth, soul-stirring honesty, and unflinching transparency, Elder Grant has thrown us the key to surviving one of life's worse tragedies: the death of a spouse. Few people can fight their way back to wholeness with enough conviction to preach hope and healing to so many who need a compass to navigate through dark places in life's issues.

This book is designed to be a beacon of hope and a call to deeper relationship with God the Father, as we witness His love, mercy, and keeping power unfold within the pages of this book, having been lived out in the pages of Elder Grant's life. Perhaps some of the Kingdom's best gifts have been withheld until such a time as this. Further, perhaps some pain has been divinely permitted by God and laid on the lives of certain people who, in time, would be positioned in such a way and graced with eloquence to trumpet the words of a great God who always keeps His eyes on us.

In The Potter's House Church, Elder Grant's commanding pulpit presence lifts the hearts of the people who are exposed to her ministry. But her ministry is not limited to the stage. That would indeed be limiting an immeasurable gift. She finds expression as a teacher, an exhorter, an encourager, and now as an author. Her life echoes passion and conviction that is matched only by the senior pastor of our church, Bishop T.D. Jakes.

The question that plagues so many is how to make sense of nonsense. What do you do when your best-laid plans are suddenly interrupted? The answers are not always simple. The logic does not readily take over, even from the most stalwart personalities. Life can hand you things that throw you off balance and keep you off balance for a long time. *Balance*...a word that sounds so poetic, so beautiful to have...*balance,* the golden ring, the crowning jewel of a life well-lived...difficult to obtain at times, and even harder to keep.

Elder Grant's message is a much-needed one in times like these. It teaches us that everything doesn't have to be all right for your life to be a life worth living. Perhaps the joy that we seek is in thanking God for the things we have left and not focusing on the things we've lost.

If this proverbial virtuous woman has anything to be added to her credit, it is that *"her children shall rise up and call her blessed"* (see Prov. 31:28). These kinds of accolades come from children who have watched her closely and know her pains intimately and will in time mirror the same character demonstrated in front of them in this anointed woman of God. Elder Grant's children, with beaming faces, are her continuing testimony of a strength that we will only come to be acquainted with in the pages of this book.

I am happy to have contemplated truth, weighed issues, and shared deep revelation with such a mighty woman of God as Elder Sharon Grant. Further, I am honored to have my life intersect with hers at this pivotal moment in her ministry. This is truly a defining moment in the life of a gifted vessel of God. It is with this conviction that I know this book is not just ink on paper; it is the revealing of a soul. It is a soul that has been touched with greatness and we are blessed to share that experience and be inspired by the triumph of a spirit that continues to exclaim, "Giving Up is Not An Option."

Pastor Derick M. Faison<br>
Associate Pastor of The Potter's House

# PREFACE

It has been nearly six years since I have attempted to complete this book. Years ago I began to write all that I heard in my heart, thinking one day I would publish something that would help someone else. I created and recreated this book several times on paper and in my head. However, the closer I came to finishing, the more excuses I would create. So I gave up on telling what was in my heart.

I gave up for several reasons. The main reason was that every time I read about the tragedy that took place in my life, I relived the pain in my heart. The emotions and heartache I felt, even after a few years, was intense. Each time I pondered that moment and the moments afterward, it seemed like it happened just the day before. My day would end with my heart filled with sadness and my pillow full of tears. So, I stopped writing. My attitude became apathetic, and I pushed the book to the side.

However, every time I pushed it to the side, something inside me would twinge. It was as if the voice in my head was saying, *Finish!* However, the pains in my heart said, *Leave it alone because it hurts too badly, and your story can't help anyone*. I was wrestling with my heart and my head. I wasn't sure which one was winning because it was a constant tug-of-war. I was beginning to understand what Paul stated in Galatians 5:17 (AMP):

*For the desires of the flesh are opposed to the [Holy] Spirit, and the [desires of the] Spirit are opposed to the flesh (godless human nature); for these are antagonistic to each other [continually withstanding and in conflict with each other], so that you are not free but are prevented from doing what you desire to do.*

With every fiber of my being I attempted to ignore the voice; but the more I ignored it, the louder it became. I began to tell myself every excuse I could think of. Self-criticism placed me in a paralytic stupor. I criticized the way I wrote, my thought pattern, and convinced myself that what I had to say wouldn't be a source of strength for anyone. I even convinced myself that this was not a part of my purpose—not that I even knew my purpose. I was afraid of revealing the pain, my insufficiencies, and my insecurities. All I wanted was for the pain in my heart and the voice in my head to stop. What I didn't understand was that in order for it to stop, I had to endure the pain and obey the voice in my head.

One night while I was teaching class, my students and I discussed our goals. We talked about the things we wanted to do in our lives but had always allowed something to hold us back from doing. This is when I revealed that writing and publishing this book would be the thing *I* would do…*if* I knew I couldn't fail. After the students shared their goals with me, I wrote them on the blackboard. As we reviewed each goal I asked the students what happened for them to stop working toward their goals. The reasons varied from no money to lack of education, but after much discussion the ultimate reason was fear of failure. The next question I posed to them was, *What made them think failing was an option if God chose them to fulfill that purpose?*

God never said we were failures. Often we fail because of our lack of confidence or because of circumstances and issues. However, that does not mean that our goal is impossible. Unfortunately, many times we quit before we start because we don't see the provision and the final outcome. As I looked at the creative ideas on the blackboard, I imagined the lives we could have touched. I imagined where we would be in our own lives had we not given up on our hearts' desires. Were we consumed by the fear of failure or the fear of success? Did we give up without even trying? What transpired in our lives that made us stop walking according to God's plan and purpose?

> *Ye did run well; who did hinder you that ye should not obey the truth? This persuasion cometh not of Him that calleth you* (Galatians 5:7-8).

After class, I drove home on a dark road with only my thoughts and me. I pondered the reasons why I had created this atmosphere of stagnation. Although reliving the pain in my heart was not something I wanted to do, was I really afraid of failure or success? Could I handle this book possibly reaching thousands of people and my life becoming an open book? What about the opposition that would come? What person could I have helped but didn't because I was stuck in my own selfishness? Even more, what am I teaching my children about fulfilling the purpose God has for their life? Am I teaching them to give up?

All of the questions, doubts, and fears began to plague my mind, but this was the pivotal moment in my life when the voice in my head said, *Giving up is not an option.* I was afraid; but I was tired of not doing what I knew deep in my heart God called me to do. I reminded myself of Second Timothy 1:7, *"For God hath not given us the spirit of fear, but of power, and of love, and of a sound mind."* Instead of focusing on the negatives, I focused on the fact that God was about to utilize my pain to fulfill His purpose in my life. With a willing heart and a testimony of God's faithfulness, love, and restoration I began to understand that there's a purpose for the pain, and giving up is not an option.

Every heartache endured carries purpose. And honestly it is extremely difficult to understand or acknowledge it, but God has planned and ordained how everything will work together to achieve the purpose He has for your life. You were created with a specific purpose in God's mind. Experiencing and enduring the pain work as a catalyst that pushes you toward God. The pain is oftentimes excruciating, but God promised that it will *all* work together for good (see Rom. 8:28).

It is important to know that when we feel we have reached the point of no return, it is in this moment that God steps in and carries us the rest of the way. It is the intention of God to perpetually propel us to the next level of knowing who He truly is. That is the ultimate purpose behind the pain.

At this moment you may be experiencing a season of life that is pushing you toward giving up. But before you move toward that step, take a moment to ponder the answers to these questions:

- What purpose does God have for your life?

- Do you trust God to know and plan your future?

- Is God working on you to achieve a greater good?

- Are you experiencing these struggles and tragedies in order for you to be able to minister effectively to someone else?

- Have you ever pondered in your mind why it is that you must endure the situation you face and others don't?

- Why does it seem like God is being harder on you than the unbeliever or sinner?

- Are your trials more difficult and your fire hotter than those around you?

If you can answer yes to several of those questions, that's an indication that those challenges are going to be helpful for you to truly fulfill the purpose God established for you.

As you continue reading you may ask yourself, *How can the pain I feel achieve a purpose for God? Amidst everything I have done in my life, how can God use me? Why would God not change His mind toward me?* There is an answer to those questions. Complete darkness may surround you, but there is definitely light at the end of the tunnel if you know, believe, and trust that God has ordained a purpose for your life.

Pain has a way of knocking you down to your knees, but trusting God has a power that will propel you to a place in Him that will enable you to see brighter days. In this life, there will always be pain—it's a small price we pay for the huge sacrifice He made. Still, everything that happens in your life happens for a greater purpose.

Upon completion of this book I wanted to be able to say that I achieved never being pushed to the point of giving up; however, that would not be true. But I now understand that for all of the pain I have endured in my life, behind it is purpose. I also understand that I can't give up when the pressures of life are seemingly unendurable.

As you read this book, I pray and hope that you evaluate your life and realize that you, too, have purpose, even in the midst of your storm. Giving up is not an option because with God all things are possible!

Has life ever confronted you with challenges that made you wonder how you would have the strength to live another moment? Have you ever experienced a pressure so great that you've felt like you've missed the mark and it's all over? At one time or another, we've all had those feelings. However, the question is, "How do you navigate the emotional pitfalls of the enemy and recognize that truly, it's not over?"[1]

# ENDNOTE

1. Evangelist Nichelle L. Early, "It's Not Over, It's Just Begun," PreachingWoman.com (July 2008).

# INTRODUCTION

*"It was the **best of times**, it was the **worst of times**,*
*it was the age of wisdom, it was the age of foolishness,*
*it was the epoch of belief, it was the epoch of incredulity,*
*it was the **season of Light**, it was the season of Darkness,*
*it was the spring of hope, it was the winter of despair,*
*we had everything before us, we had nothing before us,*
*we were all going direct to Heaven,*
*we were all going direct the other way...."*

–Charles Dickens, *A Tale of Two Cities*

## *Life!*

Life! It's the one thing that can certainly ensure that the words of Charles Dickens will become a reality. The "best of times" represents a period of life that exudes peace, love, and joy. The "worst of times" releases an atmosphere of stress, irritation, and frustration. The "season of Light" gives the ability to see beyond the present, while darkness holds us in our past. The "spring of hope" projects our faith to another level, while the "winter of despair" creates a downtrodden spirit. "We had everything before us" reveals how we plan our future; however, "we had nothing before us" reveals how we bury our future. These are things we experience as we continuously face life's challenges, or simply put, *life*.

One of the most tragic and horrific moments of my life that I will share with you happened when I buried my husband after being married only 6 years, 11 months, 23 hours, and 45 minutes. The excruciating pain in my heart was unexplainable. I was preparing for my recuperating husband to come home. Instead, six days later, life knocked me down into the reality of seeing him zipped into a body bag. After the service, after all of the condolences and the gatherings were over, it finally hit me—he wasn't coming back. There were no new memories to create, no more messages preached, and no more pillow talks...NO MORE HIM!

Holding onto things that reminded me of him was comforting for the moment; however, there came a time when I knew I had to let go. It was during these times of holding on to his memory that I wanted to choose the option of giving up. I wanted to give up on life. I wanted to give up on myself. I wanted to give up serving God. It felt as if my world had crashed around me and all of my dreams and goals were gone. For me, it was over. However, the one situation I thought would kill me turned into the one situation that breathed life into me. I didn't understand that enduring this tragedy would be the situation to lead me into the purpose God designed for my life.

The words written by Charles Dickens describe the seasons of life that we *all* will inevitably face. However, we must understand that we have a choice of how to handle the best and worst of times. Learning how to handle them well is not a skill that is easily achieved, but it is a process that can teach us to stand strong even in the midst of struggles.

Over many centuries, even in biblical times, people all over the world have been faced with the challenge of surviving life's adversities. Unfortunately, we do not all survive, but those who do oftentimes live with the agony and pain of their experience every day. Whether the challenge is losing a loved one, a job, or a sense of security, the pain and challenges intertwined with life's heartaches can seem unbearable.

It is during life's challenges that giving up seems to be a viable option. September 11 proved to be one of the most devastating days in the history of North America. On that tragic day thousands of men and women became widows and widowers in an instant; children were left without parents, and mothers and fathers were without sons and daughters. They continue to relive that tragic day over and over. HIV and AIDS continue to rampantly plague the bodies of men, women, boys, and girls. It is also a catastrophic epidemic that leaves women without their husbands, men without their wives, and children without their parents. In an instant, hurricanes and tornadoes have wiped out memories that many have built over years. These heart-wrenching experiences can push a person toward God or toward ending life.

Pain is the one experience that most of us would love to live without. It is the pain caused by tragic circumstances, issues, and sin that causes us to be pushed to our limits. We should never underestimate the pain of someone. While their issue may seem far less than what we have experienced, the results can still be devastating. Someone who has buried a loved one or lost all of their material goods in a fire should not underestimate the pain that someone feels when they lose their best friend.

Pain is pain, but it's sad that as a society we aren't always moved to help someone in pain until it happens to us. Our expectation is for them to move into the "get over it" stage. We cannot simply rush people through their pain, judge where they are emotionally, or push them back into a state of normalcy. With every pain, each person will experience those moments that are unexplainable. We should attempt to help them through those difficult moments—as we would want others to do for us.

Often in our society people and the pain they suffer are overlooked. The feeling of a deep, intense, and internal pain becomes a breeding ground for frustration, depression, anger, loneliness, sickness, and even death. However, God is aware of everything we will face in our lives and understands the purpose for which it happens. Though it's quite devastating to us, if we close our eyes and hear what God is speaking to our spirits we will understand that He is not trying to destroy us but work out His purpose for our life. God wants us to trust and lean on Him completely.

Not everyone will experience or know the pain of a fatal illness, losing a job, or separation from family. But God knows every calamity that we will ever face. He knows every pain there is to know. That is why He instructs us to cast our cares on Him. God and His Word are the source that can help us through the unexpected changes of life. He is well aware of how to utilize that pain to help us walk toward our destiny.

*Cast all your anxiety on Him because He cares for you.*

*Be self-controlled and alert. Your enemy the devil prowls around like a roaring lion looking for someone to devour. Resist him, standing firm in the faith, because you know that your brothers throughout the world are undergoing the same kind of sufferings.*

*And the God of all grace, who called you to His eternal glory in Christ, after you have suffered a little while, will Himself restore you and make you strong, firm and steadfast. To Him be the power for ever and ever. Amen* (1 Peter 5:7-11 NIV).

Ministering the Word of God to one or thousands of souls is one thing I want to do for the rest of my life. It is a blessing for me to hear God's voice speak to and through me in order to encourage someone else. When I accepted my call to minister, the struggles and life issues became extremely difficult and exhausting. The tragedies I faced made me want to literally quit everything. I constantly blurted the words, "I'm done!" It was as if satan heard me declare my dedication to God and immediately told his army: "CHARGE!" Not knowing how to handle the attacks, as well as my own lack of confidence, trust, and faith crippled me to the point that I did not want to minister. I did not understand how enduring these struggles would achieve the purpose of God. These were the times that I wanted to throw in the towel.

Since I have given my life to Christ and committed to the call I've frequently wondered whether it was okay to feel like throwing in the towel. I often pictured God sitting on His throne watching me, shaking His head and regretting the fact that He placed this call on my life. The truth is that I didn't always handle these issues the way "the Bible" told me, so I felt less than worthy to minister to anyone. Because of these thoughts I lost precious moments of ministering as well as moments of living. My friend and author of *Becoming Engaged*, Cheryl Thomas, stated:

> What I had with God was not deep fellowship. It was the rote obedience of a fearful child—a child afraid that she wouldn't be loved if she did something wrong; a child that marked obedience with blessing. I did what I thought was right because I thought if I were good, God would bless and love me and if I wasn't I felt His love would withdraw from me. I didn't realize that no matter my state—good, bad or ugly—He loved me nonetheless.

His love for me was unconditional. He loved me because I was His.[1]

I convinced myself that if I did not perform and act out every Scripture in the Bible that God would become upset with me. My thought was that God repented for choosing me to preach His Word. However, God's Word is quite clear. God predestined and chose me. I didn't create my own life. God had a pattern for who He called me to be and the purpose He wanted to fulfill through me. I must now be placed in the position to be cut out to fit the pattern.

> *For those God foreknew He also predestined to be conformed to the likeness of His Son, that He might be the firstborn among many brothers. And those He predestined, He also called; those He called, He also justified; those He justified, He also glorified* (Romans 8:29-30 NIV).

No one is perfect except God. God foreknew us and even the challenges we would face, yet He still chose to send His only Son for us. As Christians, we should want to live a life of obedience; however, there are times that life will hit us so hard that we will not react to it in a godly manner. Even in the Bible those whom Jesus chose as His disciples didn't always make the right choices or react in a godly manner. Many times we are too busy beating ourselves down and attempting to be right, which causes us to lose focus on the fact that we serve a God who knows our every weakness.

Our purpose is not to prove to God that we will always live right, but that we love Him so much we are willing to come back to Him and ask for forgiveness when we are wrong. God does want our obedience and our lives to exemplify Him. However, that does not only come from our outer appearance but also from the heart.

*I cried with my whole heart; hear me, O Lord: I will keep Thy statutes* (Psalm 119:145).

I will never forget asking God to anoint me more so that I could be powerful in preaching the Word of God. I had no idea when I asked Him that would entail more life challenges. With hindsight being 20/20 I can now see how so many things that occurred in my life prepared me for His purpose. I believe that the tougher the situation, the greater the revelation. God reveals more of His identity as well as your purpose, destiny, weakness, strength, and spiritual growth as you face life's challenges. Although it may feel as if you are experiencing situation after situation or tragedy after tragedy, they are meant for the good of your life and will be used to shift you into your purpose and destiny.

*And we know that all things work together for good to them that love God, to them who are the called according to His purpose* (Romans 8:28).

*My frame was not hidden from You when I was being formed in secret and intricately and curiously wrought as if embroidered with various colors in the depths of the earth a region of darkness and mystery. Your eyes saw my unformed substance, and in Your book all the days of my life were written before ever they took shape, when as yet there was none of them* (Psalm 139:15-16).

Even before the first day the world was formed, God knew the intricate details of your life. In God's book your life was written from end to beginning, but you must live it from beginning to end. Nothing that transpires in your life shocks or surprises God. He will never say oops!

*The lot is cast into the lap, but the decision is wholly of the Lord [even the events that seem accidental are really ordered by Him]* (Proverbs 16:33 AMP).

Life, plain and simple, has been preordained by God. He foreknew everything that would take place and planned His purpose accordingly. He knows what you can handle even when you don't. He allows the fire because He's confident you can handle the heat. God even rewards you with blessings of joy and peace in the midst of the storm because He knows you deserve the best.

Always remember that if God established a plan for your life before the challenges occurred, then He made provisions for you to endure. God sees your heart. He knew the tears you would shed, anger you would feel, and the times you would consider giving up...even the times you gave up! The answers to all your questions are established in the Word of God for this distinct time and season of your life. The seasons of life will direct and strengthen you toward your destiny. Just follow His voice.

Although enduring struggles and heartaches can be a hurtful process, we definitely have a healing God. God is not a tyrant who causes calamity, but a loving God who prepares us for His purpose and eternal life. He loves us and exemplifies His love through pleasant and difficult situations. Learn to laugh and cast your cares on God. Learn to pray and trust God during the rough times. Hold onto the promises of God. It is because of His unwavering and undeniable love for us that through experiences He teaches us to trust Him and never give up.

I never thought that in my life I would experience something so painful. I figured that if I lived a good life by treating people with respect, saying good morning/evening to those I met, and by attending church regularly I would be safe from extreme pain. Now, I did not think I was perfect but I wasn't a bad person. Therefore, my thought process was that I was going to have a pretty good life. Of course I knew I would face some challenges, but it never entered my mind that I would face a challenge such as "till death do us part" early in my marriage.

I invite you to journey with me through one of the most painful times in my life. This pain has been the vehicle to steer me into God's purpose. If I would have given up, there would have been no journey.

*I thank Christ Jesus our Lord, who has given me strength, that He considered me faithful, appointing me to His service* (1 Timothy 1:12 NIV).

## ENDNOTE

1. Cheryl Thomas, *Becoming Engaged: Finding the Courage to Be Me!* (Dallas: BE Books, A Division of Becoming Engaged Enterprises, LLC, 2007), xiv (Introduction).

*Chapter 1*

## My Pain

December 5, 1992, was one of the happiest days of my life. This was the day that I vowed "for better or worse, for richer or poorer, in sickness and in health, till we are parted by death." I made this vow to the man God had placed in my life, Terry Von-Eric Grant. We were blissfully in love and excited to be joined together as husband and wife for the rest of our lives. It was a beautiful ceremony. After we were married we had many hurdles to jump over but we survived them. We experienced "for poorer" when I was laid off from my job, but we survived. We also survived through "for worse" when our car was repossessed. We were meeting life's adversities head on. Our love for each other helped us to make it through the rough times. However, "in sickness" proved to be our toughest challenge, and the one I had to fight alone.

In June 1999, we moved into our new apartment. Everything was in place. The moving process was a fun time for my husband and me. We were our own moving company. This gave us more time to spend with each other and our daughters. We laughed as we struggled to move the furniture. We also reminisced on the times we had in the previous apartment. It was incredible. What I did not know was that these were the moments I would have to cherish and keep close to my heart.

A few days later our car was inoperable. Since we only owned one car, my husband rode public transportation and walked a mile to get to work. He didn't allow anything to stop him from providing for his family. One day he left the apartment at 6:00 A.M. to ride the bus and walk the mile to arrive at work by 9:00 A.M. We were only 15 minutes from his office by car; but by public transportation it was over an hour. It was raining profusely on this day, but my husband was determined to get to the office, so he rode the bus and walked the mile as usual. Upon his return home, Terry began to feel sick. Thereafter, my husband became weak, but we both thought he was still exhausted from the move and from having to walk to work.

## First Doctor's Appointment

As a precaution we decided that he should visit the doctor for a check-up in July 1999…Friday, July 9th, to be exact! My husband began experiencing a terrible cough and sinus infections on a regular basis. The doctor's diagnosis was pneumonia, but there was still something strange about the cough. The doctor prescribed a cough medicine with codeine and suggested that my husband stay home for at least a week. I thought that was sound advice because my husband was a workaholic.

We filled the prescription and followed the doctor's orders, but over a short period of time my husband became lethargic and experienced partial dementia. It was difficult for him to maintain information, and I knew something was wrong because that was unusual for him. We went back and forth to the doctor. On the advice of my best friend who is a nurse, we asked the doctor to perform a Complete Metabolic Profile (CMP). After completing the profile the doctor suggested that my husband schedule an appointment to visit a lung specialist and neurologist. He was only able to visit the lung specialist who also diagnosed him with pneumonia.

On August 13–15, 1999, our daughters and I attended a friend's wedding in Detroit, Michigan. I didn't want to leave my husband, but he said he would be fine and that we should go. My husband drove us to the airport. I noticed that he was tired, weak, and his skin was extremely clammy. I asked him if he was okay. He stated he was just tired and needed to get some rest. While in Detroit I called home continuously, but there was no answer. This was quite unusual. Anxiety began to overwhelm me, so I called my parents and friends for help to make sure my husband was okay. They were finally able to reach him on Sunday morning, August 15, 1999. The girls and I returned Sunday night.

When Terry arrived at the airport he was even more lethargic. He looked different. He appeared extremely exhausted and frail. I told him I was worried about him. He stated that he had taken the medicine over the weekend and the codeine negatively affected his system. I decided that he should return to the doctor.

Tuesday, August 17, 1999, at 8:30 A.M., my husband kissed me and said that he had a few errands to run and he would return soon. We both said "I love you," and he proceeded to the girls' room to kiss them. The errands should have taken approximately two hours; however, at noon I became concerned because he was not back yet and hadn't called. My husband would always call if there was a change of plans.

## Lost and Found

I did not hear from him by 6:00 P.M., midnight, or 1:00 A.M. Wednesday morning. I could not place a missing person report because it was not yet 24 hours. The phone finally rang at 2:00 A.M. Wednesday morning. I was afraid to answer the phone because of the "what ifs" that had plagued my mind, but I did. It was Terry. He was at the hospital emergency room. I was elated when I heard his voice but scared at the same time. I told him I loved him and asked if he was okay. He stated that he was okay, but had fallen asleep in the car and did not know where he was. When he awakened he said he could only see a large red sign and walked toward it. As he got closer to the sign he noticed it was the emergency area of the hospital. What I didn't know is that he had an appointment with the lung specialist earlier that day and he had taken the medicine the night before.

He did not sound like himself, but I told him that I loved him again and I was on my way. I called my father and sister to come over to watch the girls. When they arrived I explained what had happened, and my sister stayed with the girls while my father drove me to the hospital.

I walked through the glass doors of the emergency room and saw a man sitting with his back toward the doors speaking with a nurse, but I didn't think that was my husband because the man was extremely thin. I walked to the waiting area where Terry said he would be sitting but did not see anyone. I checked the other side and still did not see him. Then I returned to the nurses' station where I saw the young man sitting and began asking the nurse if she had seen a young man with my husband's description. As I described Terry, the man sitting in the chair turned around and I saw that it was him. My heart was happy to see him, but my eyes filled with tears because of what I saw. This was the beginning of life as I knew it going on a downward spiral.

My husband was immediately taken to a room where doctors questioned and examined him for hours. He was admitted to the hospital for further tests. This was a very difficult time for me, but I knew I had to stay strong for my family. After a week my husband was released from the hospital. It was difficult because now I was not only his wife, I was his caregiver.

## One Step Forward, Two Steps Back

The following week after being released from the hospital, my husband, the girls, and I went to the doctor for a follow-up visit. On our way there we had a wonderful time singing and laughing. My husband looked like he was getting better.

Once in the doctor's office he was administered a flu shot. Within a couple of hours, Terry began to become weak to the point that he could barely walk. When we returned home he lay in bed for hours trying to regain his strength. Unfortunately, his body could not fight the flu-like symptoms. I watched my husband attempt to walk from the bathroom to the bed, but he lost the functions of his legs and fell to the floor.

I did not know what was happening and I asked him to lift himself from the floor and return to bed. He stated that he couldn't. I immediately became afraid and confused, so I asked, "What do you mean you can't lift yourself from the floor?" My husband then informed me that he could not move his legs.

With tears in his eyes, my husband looked at me and reiterated, "I really can't move my legs." My heart sank, and my eyes filled with tears. During the next four hours I attempted to lift him from the bedroom floor and keep the girls busy in the living room at the same time. I finally returned him to the bed, and he was not able to move on his own at this time. We thought he would regain his strength over a few days so I didn't call the doctor right away. But for the moment my husband was bedridden.

After about two weeks I called the doctor's office and shared my concerns. The nurse suggested I call 9-1-1 to return my husband to the hospital. So I made the call. Then I talked to my sister on the phone and she offered to come over and pick up the girls and take care of them for the weekend. I was so grateful. The girls left without knowing what was happening, and the paramedics attended to my husband. He was in excruciating pain, and the paramedics had to remove him from the bed quickly. I fought to stay strong and keep the Word in my heart and my mind; however, it appeared this situation was closing in on me.

## *Back in the Emergency Room*

When we arrived at the emergency room it appeared that Terry was losing consciousness. While home he hadn't eaten or drunk much because of the effects from the flu and some of the medications. In addition, he was becoming a little despondent. Once in the emergency room, the attending physician began to administer oxygen to Terry. He informed me that my husband was not receiving enough oxygen to his brain. He stated that he could become comatose or be placed on a respirator. The doctor strongly suggested that I think about what my decision would be if asked to remove him from an apparatus. My heart sank and I wanted to scream….*Noooooooooo!* I cried uncontrollably because of what was happening. I was confused. I called a friend and we talked, cried, and prayed. Later, I visited my husband's room and began to fervently pray and lay hands on him in the name of Jesus. An hour later my husband began receiving oxygen to his brain and was aware of his surroundings. Praise the Lord! He was then admitted to the hospital.

During this hospital stay my husband was placed in the ICU to make sure he was not infected by tuberculosis as well as pneumonia. I spent as much time at the hospital as possible but knew I could not stay away from our daughters too long. Our daughters were only three and one year old, so they did not have many questions, but they asked where their father was because they missed him. I was hurting because there was nothing I could do but pray that my husband and their father would get better.

After a week and a half of my husband's hospital stay, the doctor called and stated that there was nothing else that could be done in the hospital. Although Terry was not infected by tuberculosis, his condition was not getting better. She suggested that because I had two small children, I should consider moving him to a hospice. I thought to myself, *A hospice!!* A hospice was a place to make patients feel comfortable until their transition. That meant my husband would be living apart from the girls and me. What were we supposed to do? How were we going to handle him not being there with us? I was not concerned about money or bills because as soon as our parents were told of his illness they relieved me financially and helped in every way possible. Although Terry's parents lived out of state, they were in constant contact and ensured that he, the girls, and I were doing okay.

After much prayer, consideration, and many tears I decided that the best decision was to allow him to stay in a hospice. The doctor assured me that the nurses would be there to make him feel comfortable. Now it was only the girls and me at home, but we were still able to visit my husband as often as we wanted.

## *Precious Moments Together*

October 31, 1999, our children, my mom, and friends went to visit Terry. The Glory of God filled the room. Terry began to minister to everyone individually. He spoke words of encouragement and ministered the Word of God to them. He spoke to our girls and told them how much he loved them. They giggled, kissed their father, and said, "I love you, Daddy."

After everyone left it was my turn. He placed my hand in his and kissed it. He began to tell me how much he loved me and that I would always be his wife. We talked and laughed together. As I stared into his eyes I told him how much I loved him and he was my husband forever. I kissed his forehead, caressed his face, and we smiled at each other with tears in our eyes. As I left the room it felt like a final good-bye, but I brushed it off as something he needed to say to me. I also began to question myself. I asked myself if I had enough faith—was I praying enough or was I giving up? I attempted to keep the faith, but it just seemed like things were closing in on me. It felt as if I were at the final stage of my marriage.

His health declined for the rest of the week. His temperature continued to climb over 100 degrees. I would visit and pray daily. Something in me knew I was about to experience the final statement of our vows: "until we are parted by death." I struggled with even *thinking* of death, but the reality was that I had to. I tried to remain strong, keep the faith, ensure the girls were okay, and continue to perform my duties at the church.

## *My Husband's Transition*

November 5, 1999, I attended a church service and afterward stayed the night with my husband. His temperature climbed to 106 degrees. I tossed and turned all night long. I struggled to pray but I could not find the words to say. I felt numb. I felt as if I were in a terrible nightmare and hoped that at any moment someone would tap me on the shoulders and say, "Wake up." But I knew that wasn't going to happen. As I sat in the chair looking at the one to whom I had repeated the vows 6 years and 11 months earlier, I knew he was headed toward his demise. I clearly heard the rattling in his chest and his gasp for every breath. I couldn't sleep. All I could do was sit and wish for a miracle.

During the night I stroked his forehead and attempted to reassure myself that his condition could change for the better. I was physically exhausted. November 6, 1999, I left to attend to personal needs and check on our girls, who were staying with a friend. There was no change from the previous night. I left around 3:15 P.M. and arrived home around 3:35 P.M. I called my friend and left a message stating that I was home to get some rest and there was no need to call me back. Right after that, my phone rang, but I did not answer because I thought it was my friend calling me back to make sure I was okay. I did not want to have a conversation; I just wanted to eat and get a few hours of sleep so I could return to Terry's bedside.

As I sat on my bed I began to say grace over my food, but it turned into a prayer for my husband. From my heart I prayed to God. I prayed for my husband not to suffer and I told God I loved my husband very much. I asked God that His will be done and thanked Him for allowing my husband to be a part of my life. I prayed that God would heal him…Amen. Immediately after I said *Amen*, my phone rang and I answered, thinking it was my friend. It was not.

The nurse identified herself and said, "Mrs. Grant…" Long pause. "…Mr. Grant has made his transition."

I hesitated. I was shocked. My heartbeat became rapid. It was as if a sharp knife protruded into my heart. I was nauseated, numb, and afraid of my own reaction. It was as if my husband asked God if he could go home to Heaven after I left, so I would not be there to witness his last breath. I wanted to cry at that moment, but it felt as if everything stood still.

## *"He's Gone…"*

After gaining my composure I told the nurse that I was not sure of what to do next. The nurse instructed me on what to do and asked me to come to the hospice. I told her I was on my way.

Earlier that day I had spoken with my best friend and she stated that if I needed her to call and say, "I need you." After speaking with the nurse I called her and simply said, "I need you," and she stated, "I am on my way."

As I was preparing to leave, my phone rang and it was my mother. I heard her voice, and I just lost it and cried uncontrollably. I cried and screamed, "Momma, he's gone, he's gone!!" My mom and Terry were very close, so she felt the pain of my heart. She consoled me with her words, and I knew it was time for me to walk through this life-wrenching experience.

As I traveled to the hospice, I stopped at a red light and heard a small voice say, "Look up in the sky." I looked up with tears streaming down my face. The sky was clear, and immediately a swarm of beautiful white birds came from out of nowhere. As they were flying I heard the voice say, "He has his wings…wings of an angel." I cried even more out of the pain that my husband would not be there anymore, but was also thankful that he wouldn't suffer and was now with God.

## "See You Later"

When I arrived at the hospice, my best friend was already there. We entered my husband's room at the same time. His shell was lying there, but I knew his spirit was in Heaven. I touched him for the last time and said, "See you later." My best friend and I stood there and cried until our eyes were puffy. Afterward, I became numb again because I thought at any moment I would awaken from this nightmare.

I spent the next few days strictly taking care of business for his home-going services. I didn't have an opportunity to remain still and grieve. I wanted to give my husband the best celebration of life. He was a man of God, wonderful husband, proud father, great son, dancer, artist, Army veteran, singer, and preacher. I wanted his service to encompass all that he represented. We were not celebrating his death but his life in Heaven. For the next few days I planned two services and continued to care for our daughters. Family and friends helped in every way possible.

The home-going service was filled with power and praise. Family, friends, and well-wishers overflowed the church in memory of my husband. It was a celebration that allowed us to praise God for his life. Before the musical celebration the next day, the girls and I went to see *Toy Story on Ice*. My father-in-law had purchased tickets prior to Terry's death. I didn't want to attend the show but knew that I had to keep the girls in a state of normalcy. It was difficult sitting in the arena knowing that afterward I would attend the musical celebration for my husband. As the girls laughed and pointed at the characters on the ice, I attempted to hold back the tears.

I survived and went to the service. Again, the outpouring of family, friends, and well-wishers was overwhelming. Each service celebrated the life of my husband. I began to understand that he had fulfilled the purpose God had for his life. *I'm glad I was a part of it.*

*Chapter 2*

# THE HOLI-DAZE

The holidays were quickly approaching, and I knew I had to muster up the strength to celebrate with my children. Thanksgiving, wedding anniversary, my birthday, Christmas, New Year's, and our oldest daughter's birthday were all in a six-week time span.

This was quite a difficult time for me because in between the smiles I would find a place to be alone and cry until my eyes were puffy. I was numb. I began to stare blankly out of the window. I entered a stupor, a daze, or a mental abstraction. I endeavored to relax in the tranquility, peace, and joy I had once experienced during the holidays, but it just wouldn't come. Tranquility and peace seemingly went on a road trip. Family and friends were calling constantly, but I did not answer because I knew I would hear one of two things: either a jubilant person with a crowd in the background saying, "Come over, we (couples) are having so much fun," or else a sad (borderline jubilant) voice saying, "Baby, come over here. You shouldn't be alone during this time." Of course I did not need or want to be alone, but the one person I wanted to be with no longer existed on this earth.

Up to this point, holidays had been days that were filled with fun, excitement, laughter, and gifts. I knew on every holiday we celebrated I could look forward to beautiful cards, coats, and jewelry. It did not matter whether it was my birthday or the birth of a daughter, Terry would shower me with gifts. The holidays were special to us whether we had money or not. During those days there were more hugs, more kisses, more "I love you," more intimacy, and everything that expressed our love for each other and our daughters. We would lie by the fire on a blanket staring into each other's eyes, using nonverbal communication to express what our hearts felt. We discovered that what our hearts were feeling, our minds began to think, and our bodies brought to reality. The deep, passionate, and intense feeling that came during the holidays was awesome. No, it's not that we did not have those feelings the other days of the year, but there was something different about the holidays.

## Thanksgiving

Now, I must face these times alone. The first holiday I encountered was Thanksgiving. In my family this is a time for us to join together and share the things that we are thankful for. Even though I had several reasons to be thankful, the ache in my heart seemingly overshadowed those reasons. Thanksgiving Day we traveled to my aunt's house for the holiday. At first I was hesitant about going, but I conceded. I thought being surrounded by family would help.

As my girls and I arrived we were met with a crowd of family and friends. The stares began. Some peered at us as if we were going to flip at any moment. They struggled to find the words to say. I thought to myself, *"Hello" would be a nice start*. After the initial shock of us being there, family and friends began to greet us with smiles and words of "I'm so sorry," "You have my sympathy," and "Are you going to be okay?" Although I'm sure they meant well, all of a sudden I felt like I could not breathe.

My aunt had been unable to attend Terry's services due to illness, so I took the videotape with me to her house. I watched the video along with her. As we watched the tape the pain in my heart began anew. I began to relive every feeling and emotion. It was a wonderful, joyful, and anointed celebration of his life but watching it left me empty. I saw the tears stream down my aunt's face and knew she felt the hurt of him not being there, but I had no words or strength to comfort her. Later I conversed with other family members. This would have been fine, except it felt like some of them treated me as if I needed medication to be put to sleep. The pain in my heart was temporarily replaced with raw resentment. They did not understand me, nor did I understand them. They could not reach me, and the pain in my heart would not allow me to reach out to them for comfort. Thankfully we all survived.

## *"I Will Love You Forever"*

Sunday, December 5th, was our wedding anniversary. In the past, my husband had always made sure I felt special. This year my other best friend was visiting from Virginia. We attended church and had a wonderful time. When we returned to my apartment I saw that there was a notice on my door, telling me that there was a package for me to pick up in the rental office. I was extremely puzzled and wondered who would have sent me a package.

I went to the office, and the assistant retrieved a long, white box with two dozen red roses, a white basket full of candy, and then another dozen red roses. I was shocked, surprised, and confused. I thought, *Who could be sending me a package because my husband is no longer alive?* I thought someone was playing a very cruel joke.

The assistant gave me a card, and it read, "I will love you forever." Needless to say I was speechless and surprised. I always knew that I loved my husband deeply. I also knew that *he* loved *me* and thought I knew the extent of his love, but when I received these thoughtful and wonderful gifts that he prearranged for me to receive on our anniversary, I knew his love for me went far beyond what I had imagined. I was overjoyed that he had thought of me, but deeply saddened that I could not wrap my arms around him to tell him how much I loved him.

## *Surviving My Birthday and Christmas*

My birthday (Christmas Eve) and Christmas Day were extremely difficult. I woke up thankful to see another day, but hurt that I didn't have my husband. I sat on the couch attempting to counteract the thoughts of not wanting to think, feel, or breathe most of the morning. I wanted to *literally* stop the pain. I reflected on the letter that I wrote to him during a pre-Christmas celebration:

My Dearest Terry,

I really don't know where to start, so I will begin with what is in my heart. I don't think that in the five years we've been married that I have deeply expressed how much you really mean to me.

You are my heart, my very best friend, and the only one I desire. I thought I knew what "complete" meant before we became as one, but I didn't. But now I know. You have made me "complete" physically, emotionally, and spiritually. I know I'm not the easiest person to deal with and that's why God gave me a strong man.

*Sometimes I sit and think about what my life would be like without you and as I'm about to do now, I cry!* You have shown me how to love and how to be loved. Even through our extremely rough times, my love for you has never diminished. When

I say I love you, I want you to feel all of the love that I have inside for you. I want you to understand that the things that you've done for your family are above and beyond what I ever imagined.

On this night, December 20, 1997, I promise that I will make every effort to make you the happiest man on earth.

With All My Love and Affection!

I didn't have a clue that the statement of him not being here with us would come true. *What do I do? How can I end this pain without going to hell?* I cried so hard that I awakened the girls. As I sat there staring at his picture with tears streaming down my face, I heard the sound of little feet coming around the corner. With one little girl on each side, they began to wipe away my tears and tell me it was going to be okay. They each kissed me on the cheek and told me they loved me. As I looked into the eyes of these two beautiful little girls, I knew that I had to survive.

## Back to "Normal" Life?

After surviving the holidays I thought I would get back into the swing of things. Although I knew this was definitely a new phase in my life, I tried to function as normal. However, deep in my heart I knew there was nothing normal about my life or me at this time. I went back to my duties as choir director and youth minister. I attempted to keep friendships with my old friends and attended different services at other churches. I smiled and stayed strong in the midst of people, but even with all of this I was lonely. Going back to the apartment and seeing his clothes in the closet was painful. Sleeping in the bed and knowing that I would never be able to see his face next to me was excruciating.

*How can I keep going when the loneliness is so intense? When will this pain go away and how will it go away? Do I marry someone else quickly to avoid this pain or walk out the grief process?* I didn't know where I should start.

I strived to start a new chapter in my life. I knew this chapter was starting out very differently. Terry and I had several close friends and I maintained those friendships; however, some of those friendships would prove to be more hurtful than helpful. Things just didn't feel the same. My pain intensified, but no one knew. I was struggling on the inside. I learned how to put on a face. I was lonely in the midst of a crowd. I attended service after service, but my mind would be in a different place. People began to look and act differently to me. Or maybe they weren't different, but I knew I was. I isolated myself by gradually easing myself out of the mix. I began to attend only certain services, and at those services I planned my escape route so people wouldn't confront me. The crowd was thinning. Friends were narrowed down to very few.

## Loneliness and Isolation

At my home church people had a genuine concern but could not relate to what I felt. Every Sunday I would receive tons of hugs and kisses, but the loneliness just would not go away. Attending church and sitting in the congregation became a routine. Finding a pew near the exit became a part of my strategy. Doing and paying attention to other things as the sermon was being ministered became the norm.

Listening to the voices in my head helped to produce anger for those who I thought were not there for me. I harbored anger for my father who was also my pastor because I did not think he ministered to my needs as I had seen him minister to others. During his years in the ministry I saw my father answer calls for those in need before the break of dawn. I saw him lay hands on the sick and counsel others during their time of need. I also saw him visit homes and hospitals to pray for people. *What about me? Am I important?* I asked myself.

I thought that he should have done more for me than anyone else because I was not only a member of the church but also his daughter. I was angry because at times I thought he wanted me to do business as usual with the choir and the youth. *It is all about the church! It's all about the members of the church! It's all about preaching at other churches!* I wanted to quit! I thought what he wanted was unfair because I was hurting and he seemingly did nothing to help me. *Why wasn't I included on the prayer list? Why didn't I get an appointment for counseling? Why did I need to continue as if nothing had happened?*

I wanted to scream, ***"MY LIFE IS NOT THE SAME! IT'S NOT BUSINESS AS USUAL, AND I NEED HELP JUST LIKE EVERYBODY ELSE!"*** But I didn't. I didn't because I finally realized that my father was also missing my husband and was hurting because this was his daughter having to endure this pain. Although that relieved my anger toward my father, it didn't help much in healing my heart because I was still hurting and lonely.

I continued to do the business of the church with my head, but not with my heart. My heart drifted further and further away. No one knew how I felt each time I directed the choir, standing in front of them, painfully aware that my husband was no longer in the choir. No, I wasn't directing because of him, but he had been a part of the ministry.

The excruciating pain tore my heart every time I would hear certain songs, and it became unbearable. After one year, I decided to resign from my position as choir director. There was no one I could talk to who could remotely understand. Being alone became soothing. When I was alone it was difficult, but at least then I did not have to explain to anyone what was going on nor did I have to talk about it. I was able to just drift away into a state of numbness.

My life was no longer the same, and I wasn't sure how I was supposed to get back on track. I felt like crawling into a corner in the fetal position. I thought I could handle just about any situation. I had endured lights being turned off, the disconnection of our phone, cars being repossessed or inoperable, and not having enough money to meet our needs. Never did it occur to me as I took the vows on December 5 that I would endure this. No one really ever gets married and immediately thinks of having to bury their spouse after only a few years. It just didn't seem right. My parents and in-laws have been married over 40 years. We have their DNA! So what happened?

I started thinking. *I survived some rough days after the burial of my husband, but now I'm stuck. I don't know which direction I am supposed to take anymore. This gaping hole that is in my heart won't allow me to move forward. All I feel when I wake up and lie down to sleep is the pain in my heart. Every way I turn reminds me of my husband. The scent of his clothes in the closet, the tapes of his sermons, his paintings, his picture on the wall, and the beautiful little girls I had with him is all I want to see. I don't want to visit anyone nor do I want visitors, but I know I can't seclude myself from my family and friends. How do I go beyond the pain that I feel? I can't stay in this daze. I must find the strength to move forward because this cannot be the end of my life story.*

*Chapter 3*

## WHAT DO I DO NOW?

The thought goes through my head, *What do I do now? I'm now the head of the household. All of the responsibilities and decisions are mine. No one is here to help me train the girls. Everything is on me. What do I do now?* I was accustomed to having my husband take care of all the business for the house. He was an excellent provider for his family and a great father to our daughters. I wasn't working outside the home when all of this happened because my husband and I agreed that I would stay home with the girls. Now I was faced with supporting our household.

*How can I write an extraordinary resumé after being away from the corporate scene for two years? Who is going to teach our girls from a male perspective? How do I handle the financial affairs left from my husband? What do I do? How can I handle all of this by myself? I don't have the strength.* These were my thoughts after the phone stopped ringing and family and friends went back to their own lives. Now I was really alone, and all I wanted to do was scream. *I don't remember signing up for this to happen in my life. What is really going on?*

After the birth of our second daughter I jokingly stated to Terry that my next baby would be a girl, age 21, a graduate from high school and able to take care of me. I declared this because pregnancy and childbirth are no joke! When I made this request I was only teasing, but I was also giving my husband the clue that I was not having any more birth children—only spiritual children. He concurred. However, what I wasn't aware of was that the words from my lips would come true. I knew that Scripture stated in Luke 6:45, *"for of the abundance of the heart his mouth speaketh."* But never did I think those words would come to life in the form of that person.

In April 2000, my youngest sister introduced me to a young lady named Tawanna Williams. She was from California and had just moved to Atlanta with a friend. When my sister introduced her to me I was in the midst of one of my moments, so I smiled, introduced myself, and walked away. I didn't have the strength to help anyone, so I decided to not even commit her name to memory.

At about that same time, my oldest sister informed my family that she was moving to Atlanta and to make sure we were there to assist if she needed it.

## Mother's Day

Mother's Day was quickly approaching, and it was a day that I dreaded. My daughters were now four and two years old, so they couldn't take me to dinner or even shop for a card. Of course, I knew they loved me, but the only way they even knew it was Mother's Day was because someone told them. Many family and friends gave me cards and tried to make the day a pleasant one. It was overall a good day. However, I received something unexpected. My phone rang later that night, and it was Tawanna, the young lady I was introduced to a month earlier.

When she stated her name I didn't remember who she was. Then she reminded me who she was, and I was quite surprised to be receiving a call from her. She told me she was visiting her aunt in Alabama but wanted to call me to wish me a happy Mother's Day. I was surprised because I didn't think that she would have remembered me, either. We talked for a little while, and I found out that she was 21 years of age, had graduated from high school, and was employed with a daycare center. The conversation was pleasant. I thanked her for calling and thinking of me on this day.

I thought that would be the end of our conversations; however, I received another phone call near the end of May. She told me that she needed to find a place to stay before the beginning of June. Out of the clear blue, I started to minister to her with words that I really needed for myself. At the end of the conversation, I told her, *Even if God doesn't answer your prayer until 11:59 P.M. on May 31, He still answered.*

What was amazing is that my sister found someone who needed a roommate at 11:56 P.M. on May 31! Tawanna was ecstatic, and I was shocked and amazed that God used me.

Our conversations continued, and I got to know her a little better. Not all of what I learned was good, but I figured I was not in a place to judge anyone. After a month Tawanna began to help me with the girls. She would baby-sit while I worked on a political campaign. We were building a friendship. Over the next few months, she really became a great help to me with the girls. If I had meetings on the weekend she would stay over for the entire weekend at no charge. I made sure that when she came over she had her favorite food and drink: ravioli and Sprite. We had some great times together, and it was good for the girls. They began to bond with her because now they had someone around who was older but who still liked to go to the playground. We were happy that she came into our lives.

Over time, she stayed for longer periods and eventually moved in to become part of our family. I would love to say that all continued to run smoothly; however, that would not be the truth. We hit several walls because what I found was that we were two obstinate, vulnerable, and wounded women from previous circumstances. The circumstances and tragedies we both endured made us become bitter, frustrated, and resentful. This had become part of us, but we didn't know to what extent. We became angry with each other over the smallest issue. The words that came from our lips were like the poison of a serpent. With each argument came degrading words that eventually led to angry fights, her leaving, or me putting her out.

These were the times that we really saw how angry we were, not at each other but at the hand we were dealt. We had no other outlet but each other. However, each time we separated I would hear a voice say, "I never gave up on you!"

I didn't want to take her back because I had too many issues of my own I had to deal with, but because of this voice I did, over and over again.

> Understand [this], my beloved brethren. Let every man be quick to hear [a ready listener], slow to speak, slow to take offense and to get angry. For man's anger does not promote the righteousness God [wishes and requires] (James 1:19-20 AMP).

We began to bond even closer amidst all of the craziness. I was there to comfort her through the death of her father, the changing of jobs, and starting college. I didn't know what God's plan was for her life or mine, but I knew He would not allow me to let her go. With each moment of us being together, it was becoming apparent to me that we were connected. I wasn't sure if she felt the same way until one day, after being with me for about a year, she called me "Momma." It was then that I realized the words that I uttered to my husband were now true. I called her my "heart daughter" because she was born to me from the words that were in my heart.

Now, I had another daughter and another life in my hand. It was a scary time because I knew I was still hurting and grieving. What should I do now? The answer: I refuel my spirit with God's Word, fight this battle, and start over because He has a plan for me in her life.

## *Time to Refuel*

One time when I was driving, I noticed the fuel in the car was low. I didn't panic but was concerned over whether or not I could make it to my destination. With each mile I traveled the fuel decreased and eventually reached an extremely low point. A warning from an indicator light blinked "low fuel." There were still a few miles I could travel until empty, but I knew it was imperative that I reach a gas station as soon as possible. I could have stopped at any gas station; however, I went past several stations because they didn't have the type of fuel I needed to ensure my car would run at its optimum level. So I kept driving. I kept checking signs to see how much the fuel would cost per gallon, which would be one of the determining factors of whether I would fill the tank to capacity or only half.

My car continued to drive smoothly, but still I knew that at any moment I could be stuck along the side of the road. Because I regularly invested in an emergency roadside service (just in case one day I needed help), I decided not to go into an uncontrolled frenzy. I knew I did not have much money but remembered that payday was quickly approaching. I finally found the gas station that I needed, so I stopped and filled my tank to capacity. I decided to fill the tank completely full because I figured that otherwise, in a few days, I would be in the same position needing to refuel. After returning to my car I began to reflect on the correlation between low fuel in my car and low fuel in my spiritual life.

When we experience setbacks, sometimes our joy, peace, or faith will diminish, but that is not the intention of God. God can utilize the signals of heartaches, disappointments, and struggles to indicate that we are running low on spiritual fuel. When the fuel light in your vehicle blinks or beeps, it's only a sign that fuel is needed to move the notch to the next level. Struggles, tragedies, and hardships must come because these are life indicators signaling that it's time to move to the next level in your relationship with God and toward fulfilling your purpose. These indicators are not meant to harm you but to move you toward filling up on the Word of God and developing patience, endurance, trust, and faith.

While traveling through life's journey it is crucial that you decide whether you are going to receive half or all of what God wants to pour into your life. God has a purpose filled with many blessings in store for you, but you must make the decision to keep going even when times are low.

There are several stations where you can refuel. The station can be your church, family, spouse, or friends; however, it is extremely important for you to choose the right station. What I mean by this is that whatever station you choose, be sure the Word of God is the fuel moving you to your next level. Accepting any fuel that is *not* the Word of God is a sure way to find yourself riding on fumes and eventually becoming stuck on the side of the road.

Take care of your spirit through God's Word in order to move forward. You need this type of fuel if you desire to operate in your spiritual gifts under a powerful anointing. And you must fight against discouragement, frustration, stress, loneliness, and depression.

Just as fuel is the substance that keeps your car moving toward a specific destination, so it is that your spiritual fulfillment and enrichment are the means to overcoming life's circumstances. Your trials are needed to move you toward fulfilling the purpose God has for your life. You will get to a point of wanting to quit, but you can't! Now is not the time to give out, because you are so close.

Just as your car can go farther once fuel is added, so it is when you get the Word of God. That is when you receive your second wind and react differently to your situation. You feel like you can make it a little farther.

## God Wants Us to Seek Him

Through these struggles God is training you to seek Him for help. He simply wants you to understand that He is the answer to your questions, the healer for your sicknesses, and the peace in the midst of your storms. God is ready for you to trust and depend on Him completely. Your trials come to make you strong, increase your faith, and help you walk into your destiny.

Although it sometimes appears you are not achieving anything or moving forward, know that God sees everything you are enduring. If you continue to endure the hard times, it will yield a payday of everlasting life that only God can provide. Do not allow these temporal issues to lessen the anointing and call on your life. God has never made a mistake. You were created for a purpose. Your life (and all of its issues) was predetermined and known by God. Stay in the fight, refuel, and keep moving in your purpose.

As I walked through life coping with the death of my husband, my spiritual fuel was low. Traveling toward my destination and fulfilling God's purpose for my life seemed impossible. I wanted to panic and give up because I reached the lowest point in my life. I kept attending church thinking I was moving forward in what God had called me to do. But as I continued to sit in the pews and ignore the Word that God was bringing forth, my spiritual indicator began to blink "low fuel" uncontrollably!

I could have gone to another church, but didn't think that I would get what I needed—not because it wasn't being taught but because spiritually I was stuck. The bad decisions or lack of decisions, alone times, and the wall I created was a clear indication that I was at a low point. Instead of moving toward my destination, I was living a life of stagnation. My life was not moving forward. I was stuck on the side of the road in a sphere of loneliness, hurt, and resentment.

The gift of ministry upon my life was now on the back burner. I didn't want to teach or preach because now, in my mind, I wasn't worthy. I constantly asked myself, "Why would God speak to or through me?" My calling to the ministry had become an illusion. Ill thoughts plagued my mind of whether I was actually living a life for God or not. The attack on my mind was demolishing what God had called me to be. It seemed as though each step forward pushed me ten steps back.

It is often difficult to see ourselves through God's eyes. God created us and knows what is on the inside. He has put into our spirits the characteristics and gifts that are needed to fulfill His purpose. But we are not always looking at ourselves through what He has shown us. Therefore, we give up on all that God has placed in our hearts. For many of us, God showed us our future when we were still in sin or going through our situation. But because of what we have done or endured we no longer believe God can use us in that area.

Perhaps God has given you dreams to start a business, a family, or a ministry but because of financial, emotional, or physical circumstances you stop believing and refuse to move forward. Maybe you have even seen God work in and through you many times before, but you feel as though you cannot make anything more come to pass. Well, you are right! *You* cannot make anything come to pass. But God, who placed the dream in your heart, has made every provision for the vision.

> *And the Lord answered me, and said, Write the vision, and make it plain upon tables, that he may run that readeth it. For the vision is yet for an appointed time, but at the end it shall speak, and not lie: though it tarry, wait for it; because it will surely come, it will not tarry* (Habakkuk 2:2-3).

Are you at a crossroads in your life? Are you asking yourself, *What do I do now? How do I move beyond where I am? How can the pain that I have endured, the sacrifices I have made, and the tears I have cried manifest the vision I have seen?* It seems impossible to achieve the dream when everything around you is the opposite. It doesn't look possible to achieve the dream of starting a business when you were just laid off or fired from your job. The dream looks bleak when you are attempting to start a ministry and you don't have the finances. During this time it is very easy to give up, procrastinate, and say to yourself, *I can't do it!* However, these are the moments that God will utilize to start the dream. It is when we are at the point of not knowing how we are going to achieve the dream that God will move in and order our steps.

God has never asked us to handle any situation, tragedy, or dream alone. He has promised that He will always be with us. Our task is simply to trust and seek God, stand on His Word, and believe that He is faithful to all He has promised.

> *For as the rain cometh down, and the snow from heaven, and returneth not thither, but watereth the earth, and maketh it bring forth and bud, that it may give seed to the sower, and bread to the eater:* **So shall My word be that goeth forth out of My mouth: it shall not return unto Me void, but it shall accomplish that which I please, and it shall prosper in the thing**

*whereto I sent it. For ye shall go out with joy, and be led forth with peace: the mountains and the hills shall break forth before you into singing, and all the trees of the field shall clap their hands* (Isaiah 55:10-12).

What do you do now? Understand that God is patiently waiting for you to come to Him for the answer. We cannot fathom all the details that must be arranged in order to achieve the purpose of God. It is through faith, prayer, fasting, and studying God's Word that we can receive His instructions and move into purpose.

Read over the following verses:

*Blessed are they that keep His testimonies, and that **seek Him** with the whole heart* (Psalm 119:2).

*I love them that love Me; and those that **seek Me** early shall find Me* (Proverbs 8:17).

***Seek ye the Lord** while He may be found, call ye upon Him while He is near* (Isaiah 55:6).

*Then shall ye call upon Me, and ye shall go and pray unto Me, and I will hearken unto you. And ye shall **seek Me,** and find Me, when ye shall **search for Me** with all your heart* (Jeremiah 29:12-13).

*The Lord is my portion, saith my soul; therefore will I hope in Him. The Lord is good unto them that wait for Him, to the soul that **seeketh Him*** (Lamentations 3:24-26).

*But without faith it is impossible to please Him: for he that cometh to God must believe that He is, and that He is a rewarder of them that diligently **seek Him*** (Hebrews 11:6).

*Glory ye in His holy name: let the heart of them rejoice that **seek the Lord. Seek the Lord** and His strength, **seek His face** continually* (1 Chronicles 16:10-11).

*If My people, which are called by My name, shall humble them-selves, and pray, and* **seek My face,** *and turn from their wicked ways; then will I hear from heaven, and will forgive their sin, and will heal their land* (2 Chronicles 7:14).

*Hear, O Lord, when I cry with my voice: have mercy also upon me, and answer me. When Thou saidst,* **Seek ye My face;** *my heart said unto Thee, Thy face, Lord, will I seek* (Psalm 27:7-8).

*The young lions do lack, and suffer hunger: but they that* **seek the Lord** *shall not want any good thing* (Psalm 34:10).

*Now* is a good time for you to *seek the Lord* concerning His pur-pose for your life!

*Chapter 4*

# STARTING OVER

Have you ever found yourself starting over again and again? Did you feel like all was lost? Did you feel like a failure? What did you do? Is it bad to start over?

When counting, every number after the tenth place takes you back to 1 on the next level. Try it: 1, 2, 3, 4, 5, 6, 7, 8, 9, 10. The next number is 11, which means you are starting over with 1 on a new level: **11**, **12**, **13**…then **21**, **22**, **23**, and so on. For me, starting over means that I have the opportunity to move forward on another level. I may experience the same challenges but now I can overcome them with a new attitude because I am not the same—I'm growing up. The more I learn from each issue of life that confronts me, the more wisdom, knowledge, and understanding I obtain. Starting over means there's another opportunity to use the wisdom learned from the first experience.

When you feel close to achieving your goal or walking in your purpose, starting over can seem overwhelming. In my own life, there have been situations and temptations that I thought I conquered, but later in life the root of the same test surfaced. Then I realized I had to begin again from ground zero. I thought I was a complete failure.

However, I've discovered that starting over does not mean that you are a failure. For example, losing weight is a tough challenge for me. I am constantly attempting to cut back or curb my appetite; however, it is frustrating when it seems as though my will power has taken a sabbatical while the temptation of cheesecake, ice cream, fried chicken, and other delicacies are placed at my fingertips. The thought of putting in the hard work and still failing is discouraging, but it doesn't make me a failure. What I must do is utilize the wisdom from my previous experience and follow David's step in First Samuel 30:6 to encourage myself. I must keep trying and not give up. I reassure myself that it is okay to start over and the possibility of me passing the next test is strong.

## Ready to Move

I never thought I would leave Atlanta, my family, and friends to relocate to a place where I knew no one and was not employed. I had been comfortable in my life's journey with my husband and children. But now my husband was deceased and I had *three* daughters. I had to make the decision to either give up or start over on another journey. So I made the decision to start over with the hope of achieving new possibilities.

In August 2002, my three girls and I loaded the moving truck and headed to Dallas, Texas. I didn't have any plans or expectations; I only knew that our lives couldn't end this way. As we traveled for 12 hours I kept telling myself that things had to get better. I knew we were starting over but didn't know the outcome. We were all excited about moving to a new place, but apprehensive about what could happen. We were taking a leap of faith.

We arrived in Dallas, not knowing what was about to transpire in our lives. We settled into our three-bedroom apartment and started a new journey. God began to show us that He was there with us. He did this in many ways, and it was amazing to see God move mountains just for us. The cost of our apartment was $1,180 a month, and on top of that we had other expenses, including utilities, car and life insurance, food, and other necessities. Although the youngest girls and I received benefits through Social Security and had a little insurance money left, it was not enough to maintain the household.

Finances seemed to be quite a challenge because none of us had a job. I applied for positions every day, but getting hired proved to be difficult because I had not been employed since March 1998. This period of time in our journey was hard, and there were times when I thought the decision to start over in a new place was wrong. But I kept looking in the eyes of my three girls and I knew I had to make it work. So I kept trying. Finally, in June 2004, I was hired as an administrative assistant of marketing.

Although there were times the move proved to be difficult, these were the times that I understood God to be my provider. Philippians 4:19, *"But my God shall supply all my need according to His riches in glory by Christ Jesus,"* was now my theme. There were times when I became frustrated or cried all night because I didn't know how I was going to maintain our household, but God would always send something or someone unexpectedly with just what we needed. Each year brought new challenges; however, each year my strength, faith, and courage to move forward got stronger. I can't say that I was where I needed to be spiritually, but I can say that I was not where I had been, and starting over was not a bad decision.

## *Difficult, but Not Impossible*

After we experience challenges and tragedies, starting over can be difficult; however, it is not impossible. All of us have encountered tests in our lives. Some we have passed and some we have failed, but because of God's mercy, forgiveness, and faithfulness He gives us another chance. Giving up when we fail to handle a challenge is not the solution to the problem. That can only develop into another problem.

When we find ourselves facing difficult issues it is a clear indication that God is speaking to us. With each circumstance there is a message of hope, trust, and faith. Romans 12:12 encourages us to *"be steadfast and patient in suffering and tribulation as well as constant in prayer."* Our carnality imposes upon us an impossibility of being steadfast and patient; however, it is with the Holy Spirit that we can attain comfort and are reminded that the suffering is working in our favor.

The Scripture in First Peter 1:3-7 informs us that we are working toward an inheritance in Heaven just for us. This inheritance is incorruptible, undefiled, and does not fade away, but it is important that we understand this inheritance will be reserved for those who are kept by the power of God and ready to be revealed in the last days. While we are waiting for the last days, the Scripture tells us that we will endure temptations so that the trials of our faith will bring praise, honor, and glory when Jesus comes back.

> *Blessed be the God and Father of our Lord Jesus Christ, which according to His abundant mercy hath begotten us again unto a lively hope by the resurrection of Jesus Christ from the dead, to an inheritance incorruptible, and undefiled, and that fadeth not away, reserved in heaven for you, who are kept by the power of God through faith unto salvation ready to be revealed in the last time. Wherein ye greatly rejoice, though now for a season, if need be, ye are in heaviness through manifold temptations: That the trial of your faith, being much more precious than of gold that perisheth, though it be*

*tried with fire, might be found unto praise and honour and glory at the appearing of Jesus Christ* (1 Peter 1:3-7).

Starting over after experiencing a tumultuous conflict is a part of the journey that leads us to becoming more mature. It allows us to take another step toward knowing that we are prepared to live out the purpose of God. James 1:2-4 (NIV) says:

*Consider it pure joy, my brothers, whenever you face trials of many kinds, because you know that the testing of your faith develops perseverance. Perseverance must finish its work so that you may be mature and complete, not lacking anything.*

One of the key words utilized in this Scripture is *perseverance.* Perseverance is the act of enduring in spite of opposition or discouragement caused by our circumstances. Perserverance is the renewed mind needed to overcome the thoughts of failing and the guarded heart needed to work through the emotional pain. It is the shedding of tears when you cannot find the words to say as well as the strength you find when the weaknesses have become unbearable.

Though there are many situations we have or will face that will seemingly take our last breath, it is the drive inside your spirit that will push you through to take that next breath, the one afterward, and so on. Each time you start over on a different level, the heat gets hotter and the situations get rougher; however, your will and determination to make it through will override all that you face. Because with God all things are possible!

The more you persevere, the more you should learn and mature. If you begin to look at past trials in your life, you will see that each time you gained knowledge and increased your faith. Take a moment now to recount the one situation you thought you would not make it through, then look in the mirror and say, "I made it!" Recall the things you learned from that event and how you utilized the wisdom when you faced other circumstances.

## *Learning From Past Experiences*

Back in October 1993, I was laid off from a major corporation. I thought this would be a position I would remain in for a long time; however, there were changes made in the department. At that time I panicked because we were down to one income and I didn't think we were going to meet our household obligations. However, after being unemployed for about two months, I saw God move in miraculous ways. All of our obligations were met and exceeded. It was then that I discovered I didn't work just to have a paycheck, but was actually on a divine assignment as well.

That experience taught me about my relationship with God and strengthened my faith. Hence, when I was laid off in May 2008, I didn't panic because God, who does not change and cannot lie, continued to take care of our needs. I also knew it was just an indication that this divine assignment was complete and I was about to be prepared for my next assignment. My reaction to this layoff was different because I had persevered through the first one, which led to a stronger faith and maturity.

The struggle of life and having to start over is not only to mature you, but will also help strengthen and encourage your brother or sister through their crisis. Jesus said to Peter in Luke 22:31-32 (paraphrased), *"Satan desired to sift you as wheat, but I have prayed for you that your faith does not fail; and when you are converted, strengthen your brother."* Sifting is a process that separates different sized particles from one another. The enemy desires to sift you. He desires to examine and attempt to destroy your life by separating you from God. He yearns to exploit your weaknesses and your failings.

However, God doesn't need to magnify your weaknesses because He knew them before the beginning of your life. Instead, He chooses to magnify your strengths and build your life on a firm foundation. Unfortunately, there are times we are caught in the snares of the enemy and unable to avoid the fiery darts. But just as Jesus told Peter that He prayed his faith would not fail, it is the same for you. Jesus wants to remind you that He has already prayed and interceded on your behalf. You are not so far away from His presence that He doesn't know what you need and will take that situation to the Father on your behalf.

> What, then, shall we say in response to this? If God is for us, who can be against us? He who did not spare His own Son, but gave Him up for us all—how will He not also, along with Him, graciously give us all things? *Who will bring any charge against those whom God has chosen? It is God who justifies. Who is he that condemneth? It is Christ that died, yea rather, that is risen again, who is even at the right hand of God, who also maketh intercession for us* (Romans 8:31-34 NIV).

Have you ever wondered whether you were related to the three Hebrew men because you made it through a situation without coming out smelling like smoke? Jesus' intercession for you is the reason you were not consumed. We must remember that Jesus is omnipotent (all powerful), omniscient (all knowing), and omnipresent (ever present). There is no way anything can happen in your life without Jesus knowing about it. He has ascended and now sits at the right hand of God to stand in the gap for you! He doesn't pray that the challenge or issue cease, but prays that your faith doesn't fail. He prays in this manner because He knows you will come through the challenges if you continue to have faith and trust Him.

Jesus also stated to Peter, "...when you are converted." The term *when* denotes that there is a period of time that something will happen. Jesus' use of this word informs us that the possibility of us enduring, persevering, and maturing is great even if we start over.

Whatever you are facing will move you into purpose and will also be the testimony needed to help your brother. In order for you to have a testimony, there has to be a test; but don't give up because Jesus has already prayed for you. Go ahead...start over!

*Chapter 5*

❧

# I Just Can't Give Up Now!

I am a fan of the *Biggest Loser* show. It is simply amazing to see people of different size, race, and background come together for a common goal: losing weight. I've seen people on the show who started with a weight of over 400 pounds and ended with a weight of around 200 pounds. Throughout the show, the trainers are constantly telling the contestants, "You can't give up!" Yet because the road of losing weight is so difficult, there are times when contestants want to throw in the towel, but then they recall their purpose for being there and the goal they want to achieve, and they persevere.

In order to be a part of the show, the contestants have to leave their family and friends for several months, with the goal of making a better life for themselves. The weight they carry has cost them precious time they could've spent attaining their goals, playing with their children, or feeling good about themselves. The decision to change their entire lifestyle is of great importance. Many come to the show with diabetes, high blood pressure, and other ailments that have been caused by their weight. However, many times the physical weight is only a sign of what is transpiring mentally and emotionally. These people realize that it is a life or death situation, and they cannot give up. Of course I'm sure the prize of

$250,000 has a little to do with their determination to succeed, but still, these people know that their lives must change drastically.

As the intensity with their training increases, the contestants now have a renewed mind to endure. It is with this mind that they push toward their goal, whether they are on the *Biggest Loser* ranch or have been sent back home. Their determination and willpower provides drive to see whether they can achieve and maintain their goal. To me, whether they win the grand prize or not, they all are the biggest losers (in a good way, of course). One of the main points in this show is that no one gives up. They are tested on every level imaginable to lose weight, but no one gives up. Although some are voted off by their peers and return home, they continue to follow the routine they are given on the ranch. For the final show, all the contestants come back for one last weigh-in. It is amazing to see the transformations that have taken place and how happy they are because they achieved their goal.

By the same token, many of us are weighed down by the circumstances and problems happening in our life. We are physically, mentally, and emotionally exhausted from trying to handle everything. We have wanted to give up, tried to give up, and at times *have* given up. But we cannot continue that mindset because we are in training to walk in the purpose of God. The routine of trying to overcome the many obstacles we face is rough. And yes, we will experience temptations and setbacks along the way; however, our determination and will power to fulfill this purpose will overcome any hindrances. A few of the key components needed to exercise and maintain our focus are faith, perseverance, expectation, and patience.

Even though we are sometimes counted out by the enemy, family, friends, and at times even ourselves, we must remain steadfast in our focus toward fulfilling God's purpose. It is great to have other Christians with us as we go through this training; however, even if we must go through it alone, it is important that we don't quit—because in the end, God will give us the victory.

> *But thanks be to **God**, which **giveth us the victory** through our Lord Jesus Christ. Therefore, my beloved brethren, **be ye steadfast**, unmoveable, always abounding in the work of the Lord, forasmuch as ye know that **your labour is not in vain** in the Lord* (1 Corinthians 15:57-58).

> *Wherefore take unto you the whole armour of God, **that ye may be able to withstand** in the evil day, and **having done all, to stand.** Stand therefore, having your loins girt about with truth, and having on the breastplate of righteousness; and your feet shod with the preparation of the gospel of peace; above all, taking the shield of **faith**, wherewith ye shall be able to quench all the fiery darts of the wicked. And take the helmet of salvation, and the sword of the Spirit, which is the word of God: **Praying always** with all prayer and supplication in the Spirit, and watching thereunto with all **perseverance** and supplication for all saints* (Ephesians 6:13-18).

> *If thou put the brethren in remembrance of these things, thou shalt be a good minister of Jesus Christ, **nourished** up in the words of **faith** and of good doctrine, whereunto thou hast attained. But refuse profane and old wives' fables, and **exercise** thyself rather unto **godliness**. For bodily exercise profiteth little: but **godliness is profitable** unto all things, having promise of the life that now is, and of that which is to come* (1 Timothy 4:6-8).

Giving up is an act of quitting. It is a choice that we are faced with when we are in tumultuous times. Quitting or taking the dark road of giving up is easy. It provides a seemingly effortless way out, but with quitting there is no victory. Giving up can only lead to a road of destruction, loneliness, exhaustion, and frustration.

By contrast, holding on and surrendering all that you are to God seems difficult because you are no longer in complete control. However, surrendering to God gives you a triumphant spirit and the power to know that you are more than a conqueror. What's your choice? Which road will you take? Matthew 7:13-14 declares:

*Enter ye in at the strait gate: for wide is the gate, and broad is the way, that leadeth to destruction, and many there be which go in there at: because strait is the gate, and narrow is the way, which leadeth unto life, and few there be that find it.*

Unfortunately, many are traveling the dark road of giving up these days. The life God has purposed for us to live seems too difficult. Christians often come close to giving up because the enemy doesn't want us to move forward toward the destiny God has prepared for our lives. Although we are very aware of what the Word of God says, we often feel paralyzed to act on it because our challenges and tragedies seem to consume our focus.

I am often reminded of Job's situation. Although Job was a righteous man, he endured tragedy after tragedy. However, Job persevered—despite not getting the greatest advice from his friends. Even though Job began to question many things, he remained steadfast in his belief that God was going to bring him through.

*But He knoweth the way that I take: when He hath tried me, I shall come forth as gold. My foot hath held His steps, His way have I kept, and not declined. Neither have I gone back from the commandment of His lips; I have esteemed the words of His mouth more than my necessary food* (Job 23:10-12).

Because of the vicissitudes (the uncontrollable, seemingly random ups and downs) of life we face, oftentimes we need someone who can perform surgery with the Word of God. Many of us are in dire need of an oxygen tank because we have stopped breathing. We need an X-ray on our heads, a CAT scan on our hearts, and a cast to support the brokenness of our flesh.

I have always heard and believed that the Church is a hospital. The Church is the place where we can be spiritually healed, cared for, and reminded that there is nothing too hard for God. It is ordained by the Chief Cornerstone, who is Jesus Christ. Within the Church are pastors, elders, ministers, as well as teachers who are gifted and specialize in several areas to heal our brokenness. They have the divine ability to search the Word of God in order to minister to the heart of the people on His behalf. God endows them with the capability to know there is no fiery dart that can attack the lives of His children that cannot be overcome with His Word. The leaders of the Church have the ability to preach or teach the Word until the mind is renewed and saturated with thoughts of peace and not destruction. God has also given certified counselors and lay helpers the ability to assist in the healing process. In essence, the Church is compiled of a body of believers who are in place to serve one another *and* to rescue a hurting, aching, and dying world. We must realize we cannot walk this entire journey alone. Hearing and understanding the Word of God through others gives life a deeper meaning, which leads to a deeper revelation.

We have a faithful, omnipresent God, and He will utilize others as His mouthpiece to help us through our difficult times as well as to encourage and love us. As Scripture urges us:

> Let us **hold fast** the profession of our faith without wavering; (for He is faithful that promised;) And let us consider one another to provoke unto love and to good works: **Not forsaking the assembling of ourselves together,** as the manner of some is; but **exhorting one another:** and so much the more, as ye see the day approaching (Hebrews 10:23-25).

## Breaking Point

Being a minister to hurting souls, I lost my passion to preach because my heart was full of emotions and my spirit felt empty. *Who would minister to me?* After Terry's death I didn't even know where I stood on the path to God. My heart was aching, my mind was cluttered, and my flesh was in charge. I thought to myself, *I can't do it anymore. Where can I run? I am sick of hurting and bleeding profusely from the issues that plague me. Where can I go?*

Eventually, I tried the place where I knew others had been healed. I will never forget one Sunday morning in January 2003, when I was preparing for service at The Potter's House. My children had decided to stay home. The weather was cold, and that is exactly how I felt on the inside. I was attending service numb and zombielike, without any real expectation for God to speak to me. In my mind I thought I was so far from His presence that there was no way He would look in my direction, but I figured being in service is what I needed to do, so I showed up.

There I was, sitting on a corner seat alone and struggling to smile at those I knew. I thought, *What if I just screamed, "HELP ME!" I wonder what would happen.* My life was in so much turmoil and I was at the stage of quitting.

As praise and worship progressed I attempted to raise my hands and glorify God. I wanted to fit in with the other worshipers so I wouldn't bring attention to myself. Although I really wanted to sit on the pew and just cry, I played the part of *I'm okay.* As the service continued, many thoughts encompassed my mind. I wanted to stay focused, but the background music in my head kept getting louder. It was now time for the Word of God.

Articulate and straightforward, Bishop Jakes began to read the Scripture referencing Peter's denial of Christ. After reading the Scripture he stated his topic, "Breaking Point." My heart seemingly skipped a beat, because I thought to myself, *This is exactly where I am in my life.* At this moment the background music in my mind started to subside and I was anxious to hear what Bishop Jakes was about to say. While I was attentively listening to the sermon, Bishop Jakes spoke a message straight from God's mouth. My ears and mind hung on every word because now it was not just a sermon, it was my oxygen mask. For a long time I had felt as if I couldn't breathe. I was empty. The words began to pump breath and life into my broken spirit.

Bishop Jakes spoke about how Peter reached his breaking point as he sat around the fire of those who accused him of being with Jesus. He explained how Peter denied Jesus three times and then the cock crowed, which fulfilled the prophecy Jesus spoke. Bishop Jakes also explicitly described how Peter felt unworthy to be a disciple of Christ after he denied Him.

I thought, *This is exactly how I feel!* I knew that God had called me to minister His Word, but now I was in a place where I denied Him. I did not deny Him with my words alone but also with my actions. I denied Him when I replaced His will for my life with my own. I denied Him when I thought He made a mistake by calling me as a minister. I denied Him when I got tired of it all and said, "I give up."

During the sermon, several thoughts and questions encompassed my mind. I felt as if I were in the sanctuary alone. I knew there were about 6,000 other people attending the service, but my silent screams became audible. My hands were raised as if I reached out for God to hold me. The tears I cried were the release I had longed for. I not only cried because I reached my breaking point, but I cried because God thought enough of me that He allowed my bishop to deliver such a powerful word! The nature of the sermon switched from Peter denying Christ and feeling unworthy, to God calling Peter (by name) in Mark 16 and Peter becoming the spokesman on the Day of Pentecost.

As the Spirit of God worked through Bishop Jakes, he spoke of God knowing what we have done, the circumstances we will face, and the manner in which we will answer those circumstances. With fervor he spoke of God's faithfulness regardless of what we have done. That sermon changed my life! It was my inspiration to know that *I just couldn't give up now!* For God to speak so powerfully through His servant directly to me was a clear indication that He had a purpose for my life. I felt as if God had just called me by name to walk in the desired intention He had for my life. As I left the service, I left with the understanding that no matter the situation, God's purpose for my life is certain. When there is a purpose to fulfill, God will use even the most painful situation to cut us into the pattern He designed for our life.

## *Learning From the Shunammite Woman*

There are times when life's challenges send us into a tailspin. They take us by surprise or happen at a moment when all is seemingly going well. I am reminded of the story in Second Kings 4 about the Shunammite woman. This woman was a blessing to Elisha by providing a place for him to stay whenever he came through the city. Therefore, Elisha wanted to give back to her in return. When Elisha approached her about her desires, she did not mention any of them. However, Elisha's servant knew her true desire and told Elisha. The one desire of her heart was to have a child, so Elisha spoke to her, saying, *"About this season, according to the time of life, thou shalt embrace a son"* (2 Kings 4:16).

The following year the Shunammite woman had a son. However, after a period of time her son died. In her response to this tragedy, we can see the tenacious spirit of this mother. She refused to give up. Although she knew her son was home dead, she decided to go on a journey to find Elisha. Many asked her, *"Is it well...?"* and she stated, *"It is well"* (verse 26). However, when she reached Elisha she told him all that had happened and would not give up until Elisha went to the place where her son lay dead. Once the man of God arrived at the place where her son lay, a resurrection took place. Within this story are four points that we must understand in order to triumph in our own situations.

1. Keep moving toward your destination and know it is well.

2. Do not share with everyone how tough the situation really is.

3. Don't stop until you get to the one who made you the promise.

4. There is always an opportunity for God to resurrect a dead situation.

## Learning From the Cross

Jesus Christ is the greatest example of perseverance, patience, and endurance through a horrific circumstance. His purpose for coming to Earth was to become a sacrifice for the sins of the world. His sacrifice would give us an opportunity to have a relationship with the Father. Jesus knew that in order to fulfill this purpose, He would endure ridicule, criticism, temptation, and pain. Furthermore, He knew there had to be the shedding of blood, which would come from abuse, persecution, and ultimately crucifixion.

*For the preaching of the cross is to them that perish foolishness; but unto us which are saved it is the power of God* (1 Corinthians 1:18).

*For even hereunto were ye called: because Christ also suffered for us, leaving us an example, that ye should follow His steps: Who did no sin, neither was guile found in His mouth: Who, when He was reviled, reviled not again; when He suffered, He threatened not; but committed Himself to Him that judgeth righteously: Who His own self bare our sins in His own body on the tree, that we, being dead to sins, should live unto righteousness: by whose stripes ye were healed. For ye were as sheep going astray; but are now returned unto the Shepherd and Bishop of your souls* (1 Peter 2:21-25).

The Cross represents persecution, shame, and abuse as well as passion, love, and sacrifice. Jesus experienced persecution through the rejection of the people, shame when He was spit on by the soldiers, and abused when He was whipped and nailed to the Cross. However, we experience the passion, love, and sacrifice of the Cross through Jesus' willingness to endure. The sacrifice was a heavy penalty to pay since He committed no wrong; however, Jesus suffered through it. He was beaten, bruised, spit on, ridiculed, and accused for all of our sins and transgressions. He was nailed to the Cross, pierced in the side, and buried in a borrowed tomb so that we could be restored and have fellowship with the Father as true children. His blood was shed for the remission of our sins. God gave His Son as the ultimate sacrifice to save us because He loves us.

Can we do the same for Him? Will we sacrifice the desires of our flesh to live for God? Are we willing to bear the cross alone and follow Jesus? Will we endure the persecution, shame, and abuse to show our love for God?

*For God so loved the world, that He gave His only begotten Son, that whosoever believeth in Him should not perish, but have everlasting life* (John 3:16).

During our spiritual walk it is imperative that we consider the Cross. Taking up our cross will yield pain, heartache, and at times, loneliness. But our cross should also yield the passion, love, and obedience we have for the Father. Jesus' suffering on the Cross worked in our favor because it provided a way for us to come into the presence of God. As disciples of Christ we must deny self, take up the cross, and follow Jesus. Enduring and persevering through challenges is an opportunity for us to proclaim to Jesus that what He endured on the Cross was not in vain. It is also an opportunity for us to give back to God what He has given to us—our lives!

*If any man will come after Me, let him deny himself, and take up his cross daily, and follow Me* (Luke 9:23 NIV).

*I am come that they might have life, and that they might have it more abundantly* (John 10:10b NIV).

Jesus didn't die for you to only exist. He died so that you might live. Even though the Cross represented persecution, abuse, and shame, it also provided a resurrected life. After enduring the pain, suffering on the Cross, and being buried, Jesus was resurrected. This is the powerful part of all that He endured because it declares that we can live again.

The resurrection proves that you can survive the tough issues of life. You will win if you don't quit! Jesus had every opportunity to give up, but He didn't. When Jesus prayed in the Garden of Gethsemane for God to *"remove this cup from Me,"* in His humanness He wanted it to pass; however, He knew there was purpose for the pain of persecution, abuse, and the Cross. Therefore, His next words were *"nevertheless not My will, but Thine, be done"* (Luke 22:42 NIV).

Jesus could have stopped the persecution, abuse, and even death at any time; but He chose to endure to the end because He knew that in three days His resurrection would take place and

God's purpose would be fulfilled. We serve an awesome God who has the power to resurrect a dead situation, but we cannot give up.

*That I may know Him, and the power of His resurrection, and the fellowship of His sufferings, being made conformable unto His death; if by any means I might attain unto the resurrection of the dead* (Philippians 3:10-11).

What does the Cross mean to you? What does it represent in your life? It can be intimidating to receive the fullness of God because everything about Him is enormous. However you have the right and privilege to make what Jesus endured on the Cross personal. This is about you! Instead of viewing Jesus' crucifixion as a sacrifice He did for the sins of the world, make it a sacrifice He did just for you. Following Jesus is a very expensive walk because you're in His will; therefore, the plans you set for yourself are void. The cost of the Cross is one that will take you through many tribulations, but it also offers great gain.

My encouragement to you is to continue to hold on to the promises of God. Begin to encourage yourself by speaking those things that have not yet manifested. Truth is, it won't always be easy, and you may ask God to allow this situation to pass, but know that your omniscient God has the perfect plan and purpose for your life.

Some things will die along the way as you fulfill the purpose of God. However, there are things that may appear to be dead (i.e., relationships, dreams, etc.), but God will bring resurrection because He promised it to you.

*For all the promises of God in Him are yea, and in Him Amen, unto the glory of God by us* (2 Corinthians 1:20).

*Chapter 6*

◈

# FULLY COMMITTED

*Wherefore let them that suffer according to the will of God commit the keeping of their souls to Him in well doing, as unto a faithful Creator* (1 Peter 4:19).

◈

In marriage, a vow of commitment is made during the wedding ceremony. "I do" are two very powerful words. Those words signify commitment and promise by oath. The word "I" signifies that no one else made the commitment for you. The word "do" indicates that you will perform, execute, or carry out the promise you made. As my husband and I stood before God and witnesses at our wedding ceremony, we made a commitment to carry out the agreement we made to each other. Although it was difficult at times, we chose as individuals to keep the commitment even during the challenges because we knew the best was yet to come.

"For better or worse," "for richer or poorer," "in sickness and in health" are promises two people make in marriage. The pendulum continues to swing in each direction throughout the marriage. These are the vows that are usually stated to seal the marriage. They represent the commitment each person has for the other. On their wedding day, as the bride and groom repeat those words to each other, they are blissfully in love and have not really ascertained all that is engulfed in those words. Yet the commitment they make should be unconditional.

By the same token, when we accept Christ, we are promising to commit ourselves *to* Him, put our trust *in* Him, and enter a covenant relationship *with* Him. We cannot say, *Lord, I will serve You only if everything goes according to my plan, and only if You bless me.* Our commitment is to be unconditional. Yet sometimes, when we experience difficult situations, our commitment is hard to maintain. Although we promised God that we would serve Him through good and bad, we sometimes change our minds when life seems overwhelming.

Our commitment was meant to last throughout our lifetime, but unfortunately, we have two persons living inside of us at times. During the good times we display our best attitude of praise and worship to God. It is throughout these times that God can easily get our attention and we are focused on God's purpose for our life. At those moments, our commitment and faith seem unshakable.

However, as we experience bad times, we become apathetic. Our behavior becomes irreverent, and our display of praise and worship becomes scarce. It is not always our intention to display this behavior, but oftentimes we are devastated with the pressures we face.

*Commit thy works unto the Lord, and thy thoughts shall be established* (Proverbs 16:3).

Throughout my marriage, when things were smooth I was a good wife. It was quite easy to smile during those times. I would speak of my commitment to my husband with confidence and assurance. We would exemplify the perfect couple, and it looked as if we didn't have a care in the world because we were together.

Every answer was given with a smile. We held hands as if we were still dating. We were preaching and teaching the Word of God together with a fire in our spirits. It was as if our marriage couldn't be shaken.

But as we experienced the bad times, a spirit of discord continued to disrupt our unity and cause a breakdown in our commitment. This is when we failed to even pay attention to God. It caused us to question God, cease from focusing on our gifts, and lose our praise. Often this was when I turned into Dr. Jekyll and Mrs. Hyde. There were times my husband didn't know who he was going to meet. Instead of speaking with an eloquent tone, I allowed the sounds of discontent to gush forth from my lips. My flesh would react in a manner that my spirit didn't line up with. My faith would be shaken, and I wanted to change my answer from "I do" to "I did."

> *Better is it that thou shouldest not vow, than that thou shouldest vow and not pay* (Ecclesiastes 5:5).

This made me think about the commitment I made to God one night at Wesleyan College in Macon, Georgia. I knew it was important for me to attend church regularly because that is what I was brought up to do. However, what I didn't know is that attending church would not automatically mean I was committed to God's plan and purpose. Unfortunately, I became one of the people in church who would show up every Sunday, clap my hands, and praise the Lord until I convinced myself that I had a true relationship with God. It was not until I attended a seminar in February 1984 that I realized what I had was tradition, not a committed relationship. After leaving that seminar I went to my dorm room, fell to my knees, and asked God to come into my life. I no longer wanted to only show up on Sunday and act as if I had a relationship, but I wanted to be totally committed in word and deed.

Years later, after the death of my husband, I wasn't as committed as I had promised God I would be. I lost my hope, faith, and joy. I began to do some of the things that I did before. If God and I took the vows that we do in a marriage ceremony, then I didn't keep my end of the promise. I messed up. But one day after doing a self-check, I knew I needed to come back to God. Therefore, I bowed down before Him, asked for forgiveness, and recommitted my life to Him.

From now on, even when the times are difficult, I choose to stay with God—whether I am going through better or worse, richer or poorer, or experiencing sickness or health.

> Yet the children of thy people say, The way of the Lord is not equal: but as for them, their way is not equal. When the righteous turneth from his righteousness, and committeth iniquity, he shall even die thereby. But if the wicked turn from his wickedness, and do that which is lawful and right, he shall live thereby. Yet ye say, The way of the Lord is not equal. O ye house of Israel, I will judge you every one after his ways (Ezekiel 33:17-20).

Our commitment to God is extremely important to our lives and to fulfilling God's purpose. God is always committed to us through "for better and for worse" times. When He endured the Cross, Jesus sacrificed Himself for our sins! The sacrifice He made was because of God's commitment and love for us. He gave us the power to get through any situation, including "for better or worse" and "richer or poorer." We are married to God, and He expects us to be committed to the relationship through the bad times as well as the good. Our God is the bridegroom and we (those who have accepted Him) are the bride.

Why is it that we are not willing to endure the hard times? There are times when you may not agree with your spouse or a friend, but if you are committed to them, you will endure and learn to agree to disagree.

> *Delight thyself also in the Lord: and He shall give thee the desires*
> *of thine heart. Commit thy way unto the Lord; trust also in Him;*
> *and He shall bring it to pass* (Psalm 37:4-5).

Trust, fidelity, and love are important to a relationship, but commitment is just as important. Have you ever experienced distrust, infidelity, or a broken heart? The deciding factor after this experience is whether you are committed to persevere through the rough times. You decide whether you are willing to commit through counseling, rehabilitation, or salvation. It is in the same manner that God was so committed to us that He sent His Son to shed blood for the remission of our sins. Even before we accepted God as our Father, He committed His only begotten Son, Jesus Christ, to shed His blood for our sins. God knew that we couldn't pay such a heavy penalty, so He paid for us. Talk about commitment!

> *But God commendeth His love toward us, in that, while we were*
> *yet sinners, Christ died for us* (Romans 5:8).

When Jesus decided to walk the road leading to His own crucifixion, He didn't experience richer or better, but endured poorer and worse. He was rich, with every right to sit in Heaven with His Father, but chose to become poor and make the ultimate sacrifice for us.

> *For ye know the grace of our Lord Jesus Christ, that, though He*
> *was rich, yet for your sakes He became poor, that ye through His*
> *poverty might be rich* (2 Corinthians 8:9).

## Spiritual Adultery

Being married to God is an opportunity to show our faithfulness to Him through a relationship. However, I believe at times we commit spiritual adultery. Every Christian has or will experience spiritual adultery, and it occurs more often than we'd like to admit. Adultery in a natural or spiritual relationship is defined as unfaithfulness, and often it occurs because we feel or think we are not getting all that's needed in the relationship. Adultery in a natural relationship can occur from either party. However, in a spiritual relationship, we are the only ones who will commit adultery. God is always faithful in every aspect of the relationship.

In the natural, when a spouse commits adultery, he or she breaks the trust of the relationship. By the same token, when we commit spiritual adultery, we begin to place other things and people before God and break the commitment. The children of Israel committed spiritual adultery when they decided to build a molten calf to worship when Moses was on the mountain to receive instructions from God (see Exod. 32:1-8). God was angry with Israel, but He didn't give up on them. By the same token we cannot give up on ourselves or others when we break the commitment we have with God.

God's commitment to us is everlasting, but our loyalty to Him is limited. Why is that? It is because we often endure the trials for only a moment before we begin to murmur and complain. We need to remember that the adversity we face is only temporary! If we must endure a situation that lasts longer than we expect, or if we cannot "name it and claim it," spin around three times, or use some other quick fix, then we are ready to give up!

Giving up on life's challenges calls into question whether you are totally committed to God's plan for your life. The vicissitudes of everyday circumstances can cause a strain on your life, but it is important that you become tenacious enough to hold on to God's promises and understand that the trial will not last forever.

> *For our light **affliction**, which is **but for a moment**, worketh for us a far more exceeding and eternal weight of glory; while we look not at the things which are seen, but at the things which are not seen: for the **things which are seen are temporal**; but the **things which are not seen are eternal** (2 Corinthians 4:17-18).*

From time to time we react angrily toward the people we love and trust—especially when they hurt us. However, when we hurt God, we don't seem to have any remorse for our actions but, rather, excuses. How do you think He feels when you give excuses for your actions? We tend to excuse our complaining, murmuring, and frustrations, and fail to thank God for forgiving us. I understand there are situations that are so frustrating that naturally your carnality will force you into worry, hurt, or pain. Still, there comes a time when your walk with God and your faith in Him overshadows the worry. You have to know that trusting God and yielding your mind and spirit to Him is your only option to overriding your selfishness and carnality. Commitment in any relationship yields confidence that you are willing to walk through situations because you want the relationship to last. And I want to stress the words "walk through." God never intends for us to "stay in" a lonely and dismal place.

> *Yea, though I **walk through** the valley of the shadow of death, I will fear no evil: for Thou art with me; Thy rod and Thy staff they comfort me (Psalm 23:4).*

When we decide to walk through the low places of life with our faith and trust in God, we override what our flesh desires. As we experience the hard times of life with God, His will for our lives becomes ours. His desire and purpose for our lives become our main focus. We are now beginning to walk through the times of shedding and denying our flesh so that we can live a saved, sanctified (set apart), and focused life for Him.

With every fiber of our being we must avoid trying to be our own guide because it only leads us to a place of destruction, confusion, worry, and frustration. I encourage you to hold on to the word that God has spoken in your life. Walk through the valleys, fight through the adversity, hear the gossip, and be persecuted for righteousness' sake, and in the end, if you faint not, you win–because God has a purpose for your life.

> *I will lift up mine eyes unto the hills, from whence cometh my help. My help cometh from the Lord, which made heaven and earth* (Psalm 121:1-2).

> *Blessed are ye, when men shall revile you, and persecute you, and shall say all manner of evil against you falsely, for My sake* (Psalm 5:11).

I encourage you also to lift up your head–because, after all, your strength comes from above. God's strength is made perfect in your weakness (see 2 Cor. 12:9). Look into your past and realize that while you were weak and tired, God's strength carried you through–and it always will carry you through. It is not by chance that you survived the tragedies that you thought would kill you–it was the plan of God. Do not be deceived, it's not a mistake that you lived through attempted suicide–it was the plan of God. You didn't lose your mind and get swallowed up in the disappointments of life because–it was the plan of God. The plan of God was predetermined for your life, and even though the fiery darts are hard to dodge, the plan of God is perfect and complete. He knows exactly the test needed for the testimony. Revelation 12:10a (NIV) says, *"And they overcame him by the blood of the Lamb, and by the word of their testimony."*

The enemy understands that his time is short. Yet sometimes it seems as if his impetuous tactics of forming weapons to discourage and accuse you are endless. Satan is the accuser of the brethren and will pursue you with various attacks to persuade you to curse God and give up. However, the weapon that the enemy meant for evil, God will utilize it for His good.

> *No weapon that is formed against thee shall prosper; and every tongue that shall rise against thee in judgment thou shalt condemn. This is the heritage of the servants of the Lord, and their righteousness is of Me, saith the Lord* (Isaiah 54:17).

God never told us that every moment in our lives would be good, but what He did promise is that whatever challenge we face, it will all work out for good. He knows the end result. Did you know that God allows some situations in order to mold your character? The Bible encourages us in James 1:2-3 to be patient and to count it all joy when the distress of trials and temptations challenges you, because ultimately they will mature you! As the old saying goes, "What doesn't kill you makes you stronger."

Every seed that goes in the ground must die before it reaches maturity. When the seed of God's Word is deposited in your spirit, it is the trials and tribulations that cause that seed to connect to your spirit, but it also causes your flesh to die. As your flesh dies and your spirit matures, your character will develop and blossom into fruit—the fruit of the Spirit.

> *But the fruit of the Spirit is love, joy, peace, longsuffering, gentleness, goodness, faith, meekness, temperance: against such there is no law. And they that are Christ's have crucified the flesh with the affections and lusts. If we live in the Spirit, let us also walk in the Spirit* (Galatians 5:22-25).

Your attitude, mercy toward others, decisions, and reactions to life will begin to change. Haven't you noticed a difference in your behavior today compared to "back then"? Your tolerance is strengthened and your endurance is stronger! You no longer lash out at your co-workers, but hold your peace. You no longer curse your children with negative words, but speak into them words of wisdom and encouragement.

When you ask God for patience, He will not just give it to you. He will allow life challenges to come in your life where you must learn to be patient. God already knows you can survive those times even when you don't. In the end, we come out with what we asked for and God receives the glory. It is through the simple walks of life that the ground of your spirit is cultivated and maturity is fully developed to have committed a life.

> *But he that received seed into the good ground is he that heareth the word, and understandeth it; which also beareth fruit, and bringeth forth, some an hundredfold, some sixty, some thirty* (Matthew 13:23).

*Chapter 7*

ぷ

# TRAPPED BY THE CONFLICT

*What causes fights and quarrels among you?*
*Don't they come from your desires that battle within you?*
(James 4:1 NIV)

ぷ

Since moving to Texas, I have seen God move in miraculous
ways for us. Although we have faced many challenges, God has
delivered us through them all. I am watching my girls grow up
to be young women of God, achieve educationally, and move
into their purpose. We purchased our first home and are now
feeling like we have moved from *Good Times* to *The Jeffersons*.
Even amidst the challenges, we have a closer bond and are there
for each other. My girls understand that I am not perfect, but
that I love God with my whole heart and will attempt to live life
to the fullest. However, there's one more person I need to convince that I am where God wants me to be. I need to convince
this person that things may not be happening according to their
plan, but it's happening one day at a time according to God's
plan. You may ask why I need to convince anyone because, after
all, it's my life. No one else should really matter. Well, you're

right. But this person is extremely important, and if I can't convince her to keep moving toward fulfilling the purposes of God, then everything goes to pieces. So, that is why I am adamant about convincing this person that she is moving in the right direction of who God called her to be. The person I need to convince is me!

Am I having an out-of-body experience, or am I in serious need of conflict resolution? This constant dichotomy between my spirit and flesh is attempting to hinder me from completing the work of God. There is constantly a war going on between what I want to do and what I don't want to do. My brain is working overtime and at times straining to make the right decision. I feel like Almond Joy and Mounds—sometimes I feel like a nut and sometimes I don't. What I don't understand is why this battle is so fierce, and winning seems totally out of the question. Even when I make the right decision, I feel like I am lost! I am in a conflict.

This contradiction between who I was and who I am, or between what I want to do and what I do, is causing me to feel trapped. I feel as if I am torn between two ideals of who I am and know that eventually I have to choose. The part of me I don't need to obey is the one I'm having the most difficult time avoiding. The part of me that should come under subjection to the Holy Spirit is the one that keeps hitting me so hard that I feel like I have a concussion.

I can't truthfully say that the thing I don't want to do doesn't satisfy my flesh, because it does. However, this thing is not good for me. My mind becomes overwhelmed with trying to make a decision. For many, this decision is quite easy. However, there's a battle going on within me, and I wonder if there is anybody fighting on my behalf. Because if I'm fighting alone, the war is lost! I'm stuck in a trap between my flesh and spirit.

*I do not understand what I do. For what I want to do I do not do,
but what I hate I do. I know that nothing good lives in me, that is,
in my sinful nature. For I have the desire to do what is good, but I
cannot carry it out. For what I do is not the good I want to do; no,
the evil I do not want to do—this I keep on doing. What a wretched
man I am! Who will rescue me from this body of death? Thanks be
to God—through Jesus Christ our Lord!* (Romans 7:15, 18-19,
24-25 NIV)

I consider myself blessed when God uses me to minister the
Word. I have had wonderful opportunities to travel and minister
the Word of God, facilitate workshops, and teach classes, but at
times I still feel extremely unworthy to even speak His Word.
Somewhere deep inside me is still the conflict. However, I have
learned that the more I study God's Word, the less I give in to the
conflict in my flesh.

I remember several times when I was ministering the Word of
God and during the sermon God would allow me to illustrate
points through the conflicts I experienced. I'm not eager to tell others of the bad decisions I have made or things about my past, but
if it will help someone else change their walk with God, then that
is what I will do. However, sometimes this conflict puts me in an
area of feeling guilty, and one of things that I don't want to do is
preach guilty. I want to live my life for God to where, when I
preach, then I am not guilty of the things that God will have me to
deliver to His people, but this conflict is ever present.

As I was reading the Word of God I noticed that even Jesus'
disciples and those He chose to fulfill His purpose were trapped by
conflicts. One that particularly drew my attention was Peter. Peter
was one of Jesus' disciples who had revelation knowledge and was
a devout follower. Nonetheless, Peter was faced with a conflict. In
Matthew 16:16-17, Peter had a revelation from God of who Jesus
was. Because of what was revealed in his spirit, Peter stated that

Jesus was the Christ, Son of the living God (see Matt. 16:16). However, in Matthew 26 Jesus tells Peter that he will deny Him three times before the cock crows, but Peter tells Jesus he will *not* deny Him. Yet we can see the conflict between what Peter's spirit knows and what his flesh does arises in the latter verses of Matthew 26. Peter even becomes indignant as three people accuse him of knowing and being with Jesus. After Peter recognized what he had done and remembered the words of Jesus, the guilt and shame of denying Jesus led to him weeping bitterly. Peter knew what he wanted to do, but the thing he did not want to do prevailed. Even though Peter denied Jesus, it was a part of the plan to fulfill the purpose of God.

Have you ever had a fight with yourself? Now, before you try to commit me to a psychiatric ward, think about it. You are mind, body, and spirit. Has there ever been a time in your life where your mind and spirit didn't agree? And when you finally made the decision to choose between the action of your mind or your spirit, your body would make it a reality. Have you ever wrestled with the thoughts in your mind and the Word in your spirit? This is the conflict that so many of us endure. This conflict creates discord, inconsistencies, and tension. It forms an opposition because the desires, needs, or impulses are incompatible and contradictory one to another. This conflict can occur in a physical, spiritual, mental, or emotional state. When the conflict arises it definitely forces you into a difficult area of decision making.

## My Conflict

I had been unemployed for almost nine months and I was close to feeling worthless. I was at home constantly sending out resumés and cover letters, only to get an email stating that another candidate had been chosen, or sometimes getting no response at all. The mental conflict that I battled was the fact that I didn't have a steady income while I constantly reminded myself that Second Thessalonians 3:10b says, *"If any would not work, neither should he eat."* My mind steadily focused on the fact that I was taking care of the entire household; therefore, I needed to find employment. But my spirit reminded me that God has a plan for my life and is preparing me for my next assignment. This battle made me feel as if I were on a seesaw. It was a war between my faith and my reality. There was always a constant conflict. My desires, needs, or impulses were not matching what I heard in my spirit. My spirit said wait on the Lord and be of good courage, but my flesh said you need to make it happen now or you will lose everything! Although it was difficult at times, I waited patiently and knew that God, who never changes, would see us through.

> *I had fainted, unless I had believed to see the goodness of the Lord in the land of the living. Wait on the Lord: be of good courage, and He shall strengthen thine heart: wait, I say, on the Lord* (Psalm 27:13-14).

With this constant struggle I often gave up trying to fight the war between my flesh and spirit. I felt tired of doing good then doing bad. I became a swing going back and forth. I knew I had to get to a moment where I made a concrete decision. I had to decide which side I would satisfy.

It is time for us to walk in the life that God has called us to. If we continue to speak negative words over our life, yield to the temptations, or focus on the circumstances, then eventually that is who we become. What we say from our mouths, yield to, or give our attention to eventually becomes the direct result of what is happening in our life. For instance, we cannot keep speaking "I'm broke" with our mouths and expect to become rich! It is very important that what we speak falls in line with what is in our heart.

The Bible states in Matthew 12:34b, *"For out of the abundance of the heart the mouth speaketh."*

Being trapped by the conflict does not move us toward victory, but into defeat. We must remind ourselves of the word God has spoken over our lives. If we continue to allow ourselves to be trapped by the conflicts, the enemy will utilize those conflicts to hinder us from doing the will of God.

> *A man's [moral] self shall be filled with the fruit of his mouth; and with the consequence of his words he must be satisfied [whether good or evil]. Death and life are in the power of the tongue, and they who indulge in it shall eat the fruit of it [for death or life]* (Proverbs 18:20-21 AMP).

As Christians, we are to live a holy life. First Peter 1:15-16 says, *"But as He which hath called you is holy, so be ye holy in all manner of conversation; because it is written, Be ye holy; for I am holy."* Although there is conflict that arises in us, we are commanded to be holy. We are commanded to be consecrated and sanctified. Holiness is not an option; it is a direct command from God. He wants us to live a life that is pleasing to Him even when we are faced with conflict. However, He also understands that we will not always rise above the conflict. The Bible states in Proverbs 24:16 (AMP), *"For a righteous man falls seven times and rises again, but the wicked are overthrown by calamity."* If we fall, God requires us to confess and repent of those things we allowed to create a trap in our lives.

> *Furthermore then we beseech you, brethren, and exhort you by the Lord Jesus, that as ye have received of us how ye ought to walk and to please God, so ye would abound more and more. For God hath not called us unto uncleanness, but unto holiness* (1 Thessalonians 1:1,7).

> *If we confess our sins, He is faithful and just to forgive us our sins, and to cleanse us from all unrighteousness* (1 John 1:9).

*Godly sorrow brings repentance that leads to salvation and leaves no regret, but worldly sorrow brings death* (2 Corinthians 7:10 NIV).

## Our Mind Is a Battlefield

Conflict resides within us and oftentimes begins within our minds. Our mind is a battlefield for the conflict in our flesh and spirit. The thoughts that are produced in our minds are either toward God or against God. We are instructed in Romans 12:2 to renew our mind so that we may prove the perfect will of God. In order to renew our mind we must make the decision to not conform or take on the characteristics of the world, but instead to transform or convert our character, attitude, and decisions.

The enemy desires to kill you through the thoughts in your mind. He does not tell your hand to slap your co-worker, but he gives the suggestive thought in your mind. He suggests in your mind that this person has been attacking you for a long time and that you should not take it any longer. Then you have to decide to either obey your flesh, which will slap your co-worker, or obey your spirit, which says that vengeance belongs to God. We have the option to conform or transform. The conflict comes from the thought that has been placed in your mind, and the resolution is obtained once you make the decision of how to respond.

> *For they that are after the flesh do mind the things of the flesh; but they that are after the Spirit the things of the Spirit.*
>
> *For to be carnally minded is death; but to be spiritually minded is life and peace.*
>
> *Because the carnal mind is enmity against God: for it is not subject to the law of God, neither indeed can be.*
>
> *So then they that are in the flesh cannot please God.*

*But ye are not in the flesh, but in the Spirit, if so be that the Spirit of God dwell in you. Now if any man have not the Spirit of Christ, he is none of His.*

*And if Christ be in you, the body is dead because of sin; but the Spirit is life because of righteousness.*

*But if the Spirit of Him that raised up Jesus from the dead dwell in you, He that raised up Christ from the dead shall also quicken your mortal bodies by His Spirit that dwelleth in you.*

*Therefore, brethren, we are debtors, not to the flesh, to live after the flesh.*

*For if ye live after the flesh, ye shall die: but if ye through the Spirit do mortify the deeds of the body, ye shall live.*

*For as many as are led by the Spirit of God, they are the sons of God* (Romans 8:5-14).

There is constant conflict when walking in purpose. We frequently are not satisfied with how the purpose that God has chosen us to fulfill will manifest. Often we create our own agenda and expect God to bless it. However, when God does not bless our agenda we are then in conflict with whether we will fulfill our agenda or His purpose. Sometimes God's purpose creates an inner conflict that will push us to the point of giving up. Because the pain in achieving the purpose of God can be excruciating, we stop moving forward. However, we must understand that the pain we endure has the ability to mature us so that we can carry out the purpose God has for our life.

Unfortunately, when we are wrestling with the conflict we are unable to comprehend how the pain of it will work for the greater good as we are experiencing it. Yet once we come to a resolution that we will not yield to what goes against God, God then reveals to us how the pain was a necessity. There is not a conflict we face that we cannot overcome. Whether this conflict is physical, mental, emotional, or spiritual God always creates a way of escape.

> *There hath no temptation taken you but such as is common to man: but God is faithful, who will not suffer you to be tempted above that ye are able; but will with the temptation also make a way to escape, that ye may be able to bear it* (1 Corinthians 10:13).

Many times as we experience adversities we underestimate the power of God to deliver us. We become so overwhelmed and plagued with unworthiness, guilt, and shame that we feel there is no way God will come to our rescue. It is then that our thoughts, visions, and purpose become a dry place for stagnation. The struggles we face move us to ask why we are going through this rough time. The valley seems to be the only place we will ever live because every moment we move forward, something seemingly compels us to move backward. We are in dire need of restoration, reconciliation, regeneration, and revival.

> *But all things are from God, Who through Jesus Christ reconciled us to Himself [received us into favor, brought us into harmony with Himself] and gave to us the ministry of reconciliation [that by word and deed we might aim to bring others into harmony with Him]. It was God [personally present] in Christ, reconciling and restoring the world to favor with Himself, not counting up and holding against [men] their trespasses [but cancelling them], and committing to us the message of reconciliation (of the restoration to favor)* (2 Corinthians 5:18-19 AMP).

## Going Back or Moving Forward

Have you ever become so overwhelmed with the vicissitudes of life that you have wanted to go back to where you were before? I am reminded of the children of Israel after they departed from Egypt. They were all right as Moses led them from Egypt to the wilderness until they saw the Egyptians coming after them. Once they saw their former slave owners coming after them, they began to question Moses. They asked why he did not leave them in Egypt to serve the Egyptians as well as why they were in the wilderness to die. The children of Israel were willing to go back to where they were before because it appeared that the enemy was going to overtake them and they were going to die in the wilderness. They wanted to return to familiar territory instead of trusting God to see them through this experience. They were trapped by the conflict of moving from where they were to where God planned for them to be.

> *And they said unto Moses, Because there were no graves in Egypt, hast thou taken us away to die in the wilderness? wherefore hast thou dealt thus with us, to carry us forth out of Egypt?*

> *Is not this the word that we did tell thee in Egypt, saying, Let us alone, that we may serve the Egyptians? For it had been better for us to serve the Egyptians, than that we should die in the wilderness* (Exodus 14:11-12).

Change is often a difficult task. It requires you to step into an unfamiliar area, which at times causes us to fear. Once we experience the fear, then we are willing to remain in what is familiar. In like manner of the Israelites, when we are faced with conflicts from the adversities of life we are willing to go back to the person, place, or thing that we have become accustomed to. Our familiar territory may be an old habit, ex-spouse, or old environment. We choose to return because it is recognizable and doesn't require change; and even though we had problems in the familiar, we are willing to accept whatever issues may arise. I suggest to you that God is ready to deliver us from many circumstances, but deliverance requires us to give up many things that are familiar for the unfamiliar.

After I buried my husband I wanted to hold on to the things that were comfortable and familiar. I didn't want to give up his clothes and other personal items that reminded me of him. Letting go of those items meant I was moving forward and changing my atmosphere. I was afraid to allow that to happen because I thought it would dishonor my husband's memory, as well as open a door that I was not ready to walk through. Though I wanted to move forward, I wanted to do so with the same ideals, thoughts, and things that were promised between my husband and me. I didn't think I was ready to experience a different life. Although it was painful, I tried to surround myself with people, places, and things that made me feel I was still in the place of familiarity. Changing these areas was one of the most difficult things to do because I didn't know what the outcome would be.

Sadly, we become comfortable in doing the same thing over and over, but the shocking part is that we expect different results. There is no way that we can plant an apple seed and produce an orange! Conflict happens when we fail to take the opportunity to change, make a decision, and stick with it. At times our indecisiveness causes us to be torn between two opinions or ideals that are opposite. Whether it is spiritual, emotional, or physical we must make a stern decision that will lead us to fulfill the purpose of God.

Even if you decide not to follow God's purpose, at least make a decision. Don't try to straddle the fence. In Revelation 3:15-16 (paraphrased), God says to the church of Laodicea that He wishes they were either hot or cold, but because they chose to be lukewarm, He will spit them out of His mouth. We cannot serve two opposing forces.

It is sad that many times we are in conflict because we are trying to fit in with every group. We play so many different characters that we become unsure of who we really are. Time and again in the Church we put on the mask to cover up our imperfections.

We feel that if people become aware of the struggles in our lives, we will not be considered as a high-ranking member in the Kingdom of God. Of course, our imperfections may become a topic of discussion for some people, but we must remember that the struggle is our strength! If there were no struggles or adversities, we wouldn't know God for who He is in our life.

Living a life for Christ involves remaining steadfast amidst the situations that occur. Conflict can develop your character or destroy your soul. You will be faced with difficult decisions daily; however, the decision you make will develop who you are.

*Chapter 8*

# HELP, I NEED PEACE!

*We are troubled on every side, yet not distressed;*
*we are perplexed, but not in despair;*
*persecuted, but not forsaken; cast down,*
*but not destroyed;*
*always bearing about in the body the dying*
*of the Lord Jesus,*
*that the life also of Jesus*
*might be made manifest in our body*
(2 Corinthians 4:8-10).

Is there a resting place for me? This is a question that I often asked myself. For a while it seemed there was always a tragedy, adversity, or sin that plagued my life. There didn't seem to ever be a place of rest. My days were full of good and bad decisions, and my nights were restless. As I lay down to sleep, my mind possessed a myriad of thoughts. It seemed as though it was ongoing and I just wanted to find peace in my life.

While in the midst of confronting the conflict, I knew God did not want me to live in that way. Although I wasn't quite sure at times of how I was going to handle each situation, God always reminded me that He was there. For many months, I prayed for God to give me peace. I wanted to experience a season in my life where there was no chaos, confusion, or conflict.

It is a misunderstanding to think that when you totally commit your life to God you will be free from struggle, heartache, or conflict. It is the furthest idea from the truth. As a matter of fact, this is the time when you experience more struggles than ever. Your life will appear as if it were spinning out of control. More often than not, my life would seemingly go haywire when I was preparing to preach. It would seem as though satan and his imps would immediately charge into my world. Every piece of me just wanted to have peace to hear what God wanted to say through me. But it didn't work out in that manner. Many times a disagreement would start, an issue would arise concerning my daughters, or there would be an attack on my body. It was always something!

I will never forget the time when, as I was preparing to minister, all of a sudden my back was in excruciating pain. It was so painful that I could barely stand. I went to a friend's home and asked her to pray with me about this pain. She simply stated to me that we could pray about the pain but that this was more about the Word that I was preparing to deliver. I knew about spiritual warfare, but this seemed to be a bit much!

Later, as I sat there awaiting my opportunity to minister God's Word, my back was still in excruciating pain. But I knew that God was going to minister to someone at the service that night—even if that someone was me. As soon as I began to bless the Lord and preach the Word of God, the pain lessened. It was as if God were healing me as I glorified Him and gave His people the Word He instructed me to give. Eventually, the pain was totally gone. I thought it was quite ironic that God would allow me to minister on the topic: "Last Man Standing."

I have had many quiet days, but what I really wanted in my life was peace. Quiet days are those times when nothing goes wrong; therefore, it is considered a stress-free day. But peaceful days are those times when everything is going wrong yet your mind, body, and soul remain intact to maintain having a stress-free day. It's not that you don't care about what's happening, but you have a strong belief and faith that God is going to intervene. Peace gives you a freedom that moves you toward tranquility and away from disquieting thoughts and emotions. It is the undisturbed faith that leads to a state of tranquility for a soul assured of its salvation through Christ, and so fearing nothing from God and content with whatsoever may come.

The Bible states in Isaiah 26:3, *"Thou wilt keep him in perfect peace, whose mind is stayed on Thee: because he trusteth in Thee."* The term "perfect" in this Scripture can mean "peace" as well. Thus, the Scripture would read, *"Thou wilt keep him in peace peace, whose mind is stayed on Thee."* In researching this Scripture, *perfect* simply means "complete." Therefore the Scripture is stating that God will keep you in complete tranquility at all times and through any adversity if you continue to focus your mind on Him. He has promised to give me inward and outward peace, peace with God and peace in my mind. Because I can trust God, I can live in complete calmness amidst the misfortunes of life.

We all have faced moments in our life where we can potentially become belligerent, discontented, and unfocused. Those moments can cause us to become distraught and overwhelmed, as if we have no one in which to place our faith and trust. We fail to remember that God has promised to keep us in harmony, if we keep Him on our mind. Oftentimes we allow our minds to be weighed down with the situation rather than standing on the promises of God. If we keep our mind on the One we can trust, we will not live in calamity and chaos.

*Be careful for nothing; but in every thing by prayer and supplication with thanksgiving let your requests be made known unto God. And the **peace** of God, which passeth all understanding, shall keep your hearts and minds through Christ Jesus* (Philippians 4:6-7).

This Scripture gives us instructions on how to handle the turmoil that may plague our lives. It is part of the blueprint God has drawn for us to overcome the hardships we face. First, God instructs us to not have anxiety or worry about anything, but instead, to take the time to seek Him through prayer and petition for specific requests. After we have prayed and petitioned, then God teaches us to move forward into giving Him thanks by faith. Although we may not see the answer to the prayer at that moment, God instructs us to be thankful even before we have what we asked. When we thank God in advance, we are moving by faith and not by what we see.

Second, God gives us an assurance of what will happen once we determine in our minds not to worry but to pray, petition, and give thanks. He gives us His peace. God's peace is not the quiet times, but is the inner calmness when life is hard. His peace transcends the finite thoughts of man. It sends you into a state of rest that even you are not able to explain. God's peace goes far beyond ordinary limits. We in our human state do not have the ability to understand the totality of God's peace to where we can articulate it clearly. However, it is a state of rest that we can only experience through God.

We all have walked in darkness and fulfilled the pleasures of our flesh. For each of us, there has been a situation, circumstance, or tragedy that has pushed us to the point of giving up because it looked, sounded, and felt as though all was lost. But God is very rich in mercy and has given us another opportunity to move into His purpose.

You may be experiencing a valley situation, coming out of a valley situation, or are about to move into a valley situation. No matter which category you are in, God is faithful. He is ready to stand with you, fight for you, give you peace, and love you through every experience.

Often we look back at our past and think God will not forgive us; therefore, what we are actually thinking is that He will not be faithful. But God declared in Lamentations 3:22-23 (AMP), *"It is because of the Lord's mercy and loving-kindness that we are not consumed, because His [tender] compassions fail not. They are new every morning; great and abundant is Your stability and faithfulness."* Mercy is God's way of giving us divine favor. Whether it is His unconditional love, grace, mercy, or peace, God shows us His compassion even in the midst of our disobedience.

We are blessed to serve God who is rich in mercy and looks at our heart. He sees the innermost part of you. As David was a man after God's own heart in spite of the sins he committed, so are you. David's heart was pure toward God. His praise and worship, as well as the way he sought the Lord for forgiveness, was exemplified throughout the Book of Psalms.

> *For the Lord seeth not as man seeth; for man looketh on the **outward appearance**, but the Lord looketh on the heart* (1 Samuel 16:7b).

God desires to have your mind, body, and soul, but He also wants a pure heart. He wants you to give back to Him the glory, honor, and praise that He deserves even when you are facing life's challenges. Many times we stop praising and seeking God when we are experiencing situations or have sinned. But I suggest to you that this is the perfect time to come before God because you are in a state where you need a strong tower to lean on. God is ready to reveal Himself to you. He is ready to talk to you, walk with you, and live in you through everything you may experience.

I now understand that many times I didn't have peace because I didn't give peace. There's a process of sowing and reaping. Whatever we give is what we will receive. The Bible proclaims in Galatians 6:7, *"Be not deceived; God is not mocked: for whatsoever a man soweth, **that** shall he also reap."* This Scripture simply reminds us that if we sow discord then we will reap discord. If we sow peace then we will receive peace back into our life. My questions are:

1. What seeds have you planted in someone else's life?

2. Did you reap the same thing you sowed?

3. Did what you reap change your life?

I discovered that in order for me to receive peace in the areas of my life that were in disarray, I had to learn how to forgive. Jesus stated in Matthew 6:14-15 (AMP):

> *For if you forgive people their trespasses [their reckless and willful sins, leaving them, letting them go, and giving up resentment], your heavenly Father will also forgive you. But if you do not forgive others their trespasses [their reckless and willful sins, leaving them, letting them go, and giving up resentment], neither will your Father forgive you your trespasses.*

We must begin to let go of grudges as well as past hurt and anger. Understand that what you feel is not being minimized or overlooked, but if you allow it to fester then it becomes a deeper wound. Perhaps the rape, molestation, murder, lies, or other heinous acts against you have destroyed your heart, trust, and faith in man and sometimes even in God. You're afraid to allow anyone else to get close to you because of what has happened before. You have adopted the statement of *I am going to hurt you before you hurt me.* Relationships have been lost because you are afraid you will relive the things that transpired in your past. However, God is instructing you to forgive them and trust Him. Forgiveness means that you let go of the resentment in your heart and love the people who hurt you with God's love. It does not mean that you have to be best buddies with that person. However, you need to realize that if you don't forgive them, God will not forgive you.

The person or people who hurt you may never ask for forgiveness, but forgive them anyway. Jesus said to the Father on the Cross in Luke 23:34a, *"**Father, forgive them;** for they know not what they do."* It is not an easy task, but you can forgive. Once you forgive, then your mind will be free, your soul lifted, and your spirit overjoyed.

Before you decide to give up on life and throw a tantrum, seek God's mercy and forgiveness for the things you have done. Also, seek to forgive those who have hurt you. Allow the pain of your past to become the testimony of your purpose. Do not become stuck with a hard heart and sleepless nights. God's peace can cover you and take you to dimensions that even you cannot comprehend. Then you can experience the true peace of God and handle the issues that this life hands you.

There have been times in my life that I have allowed issues to distract me from the purpose of God. My mind would be over-filled with anxiety and worry of how I would overcome. I didn't take to heart what God declared in First Peter 5:8, *"Casting all your care upon Him; for He careth for you."* I thought I could handle most of the situations on my own. Some of the issues seemed simple enough for me to resolve. However, when I attempted to resolve something on my own, it would always end in a worse state than before.

*Let us therefore come **boldly** unto the throne of grace, that we may obtain mercy, and find grace to help in time of need* (Hebrews 4:16).

I encourage you to understand that no matter how simple or complex the situation is, you must take it to God. As Philippians 4:6 gives us the step-by-step instruction on how to receive the peace of God when faced with calamity, we must follow it. God did not give us these instructions simply because He had no other words to put in the Bible! He gave us these simple instructions so that we may be able to obtain peace and live in tranquility. Of course, the vicissitudes of life tend to weigh us down and run rampant throughout our minds, but it is imperative that we come to the realization that without God we can do absolutely nothing!

The fulfillment of our purpose is intertwined with our relationship with God. Our relationship with God must remain intact so that we can hear His instructions. If we are continuously in disarray and overwhelmed with our circumstance, we will not have the ability to hear how to move forward in our purpose and will be more likely to give up. Peace is definitely needed on our journey. It is one of the most important components to help us stay focused on the calling for our lives. Having peace doesn't mean that we will never experience hardships, but it will give us the ability to do as Second Timothy 2:3 states, *"Thou therefore endure hardness, as a good soldier of Jesus Christ."*

We may not achieve casting our cares, praying, and petitioning God in every situation the first time. We may experience several trials and tribulations before we begin to follow the instructions. However, we must strive to move into a place where we know beyond a shadow of doubt that God is waiting to hear from us and wants to give us peace.

We are called to walk in victory in the name of Jesus. This is not an impossible dream! It is a reality, but only if we put God first. Fortunately, most of us have prayer partners, accountability partners, or family and friends we can call, but I urge you to call

God first. Although the love from people surrounding you is great, there is nothing like the love and peace of God.

Within the first few years after the death of my husband, I was continuously experiencing calamity after calamity. Between 2000 and 2001, I attended approximately 15 home-going services for relatives, friends, or a family member of a friend. There was seemingly no peace surrounding me because every time I attended a service the memories of when I buried my husband would resurface. There didn't seem to be a tranquil place inside of me where I could rest. I attempted to stay positive and even comfort those who were going through the grief, but after I returned home, I would again become overwhelmed with the issues I faced.

It was only when I began to follow God's instructions of giving my cares to Him that I understood peace. I knew I could not lie to God or pretend that I was okay. Therefore, I was truthful and naked before Him. If I didn't understand, I would tell Him I didn't understand. If I was afraid, then I would tell Him just that. When I came to Him with truth, He gave me peace. It was the kind of peace that said to me, *There's no need to worry about your past, present, or future because I am in control.*

> *The Lord is nigh unto all them that call upon Him, to all that call upon Him in truth. He will fulfil the desire of them that fear Him: He also will hear their cry, and will save them* (Psalm 145:18-19).

I encourage you to be open and honest with God. He is well aware of every circumstance and situation you are facing. The only way you will endure every trial is if you trust Him. God will give you the word, the person, or the experience you need to understand that He is your rock, your refuge, and your strength.

The death of a loved one, being a single parent, losing a job, and repercussions from your past sins are all devastating situations. Nevertheless, there are two words that always get me through whatever I am facing: "But God!" When I say those two words, whatever was stated prior has now been canceled. In Genesis 50 after Joseph and his brothers buried their father, his brothers thought Joseph was going to hate them and pay them back for the evil they did against him. Yet he did not! Joseph said to his brothers in verses 19-20, *"Fear not: for am I in the place of God? But as for you, ye thought evil against me; but God meant it unto good, to bring to pass, as it is this day, to save much people alive."*

When it feels as though you are getting weary from fighting and simply want to rest, here comes another surprise. Guess what? You have become a target for the enemy's fiery darts. It seems far easier to give up, but I admonish you to recall the last battle your mind said you couldn't endure; then remind yourself that your spirit stood firm, ministering Philippians 4:13, *"I can do all things through Christ which strengtheneth me."*

God has said that everything the enemy has stolen from you has to be replaced and what you will get back will be much better than what you had before. Although it seems as though the trial has come to kill or destroy you, it will not happen. God is going to utilize it for good to help someone who is facing a crisis. Once you come to the realization that God has everything under control, the peace of God will be your strength to continue to stand. As you walk in the purpose that God has for your life, understand that the pain produces peace, the peace produces progress, and the progress produces praise.

*Chapter 9*

꧁꧂

# PREDESTINED FOR PURPOSE

*Before I formed thee in the belly I knew thee; and before thou camest forth out of the womb I sanctified thee, and I ordained thee a prophet unto the nations* (Jeremiah 1:5).

*'For I know the plans I have for you,' declares the Lord, 'plans to prosper you and not to harm you, plans to give you hope and a future'* (Jeremiah 29:11 NIV).

꧁꧂

You have been chosen, and your purpose has been designed by God. He has strategically aligned every part of your life to ensure the purpose is fulfilled and that you will walk in victory. Before God formed you in the belly of your mother the blueprint for your life was instituted. You are not on earth because God needed to fill a space. You are a direct derivative of His image. God placed His Spirit inside of you, called you to live holy, praise Him, and to fulfill His purpose. You have your Father's DNA!

*So God created man in His own image, in the image of God created He him; male and female created He them* (Genesis 1:27).

Jeremiah 1:5 and 29:11 depict the thoughts of God toward you. You were not an afterthought. Irrespective of how you were conceived, you were in the plan of God. When God created you, the plan and purpose for your life was already written. The characteristics, stamina, and faith you would need to move into the calling on your life were placed inside of you. God was well aware of everything that you would endure. He was not shocked at the temptation, sin, or circumstance you experienced. As a matter of fact, He knew them prior to forming you in your mother's belly. Your relationship with God was pre-established.

Although according to Psalm 51:5 we were conceived in sin and shaped in iniquity, you were created in the Spirit of God. Genesis 2:7 (AMP) states, *"Then the Lord God formed man from the dust of the ground and breathed into his nostrils the breath or spirit of life, and man became a living being."* You were not created in or for sin; you were created in the image and likeness of God. But because of the fall of man we are conceived in sin. However, that does not negate or diminish the fact that we are still appointed by God to fulfill His purpose.

What constrains many of us from walking in the purpose of God is that we only see ourselves from the fall. We cannot see ourselves in our predestined state. We can only see ourselves from our present state. Because of our finite view we cannot fathom how an imperfect being could ever serve the purpose of a perfect God. We are stuck seeing ourselves through the eyes of our circumstances, challenges, and sins. We have made it a point to determine who we are and what we can accomplish based on what transpires in our lives. Over and over again we forget that God foreknew us, yet He still chose us.

The questions that I have pondered are:

1. Why do you think God still chose you to fulfill a purpose since He foreknew you and the issues of your life?

2. Why would He choose to use a drug addict, prostitute, liar, adulterer, gossiper, complainer, or sexually immoral person to achieve His purpose?

3. Why would He use someone who cannot seemingly control and crucify her flesh?

God in His sovereignty chooses to fulfill His purpose through us because even though He sees the challenges we are facing now, He also knows that it is not the end result. He knows that we are a continuous work in progress that will achieve a purpose-filled life. Because we see our many shortcomings and flaws we take it as being the finished product. In Jeremiah 29:11, God specifically states that He has no intention of harming us. The plan of God for our lives is to prosper us in love, joy, and peace. His plan provides what we need to endure this life. We are strangers on this earth; however, while we are here we are chosen to fulfill the purpose of God. Unfortunately, we have become acclimated to fulfilling the desires of our flesh. While God does want us to live a fulfilled life on earth, He does not want it to overshadow His calling and plan for us.

Time and again we think we are not fulfilling our purpose unless we are speaking to thousands or millions of people; however, our purpose may be to train a child according to God's holiness. As we train that child in God's way, God may, in turn, use that child as an adult to speak into the lives of multitudes. In actuality, then, we are speaking to millions because we were able to touch the life of that one child. God has released His anointing, Spirit, and power within us so that we can speak into the lives of others and be a blessing to someone else.

I applaud the many missionaries in foreign countries. They unselfishly give up what their lives could be as well as, at times, their freedom. They sacrifice to aid someone else spiritually, physically, and financially, all for the cause of Christ and His purpose.

Many missionaries are not famous, their names known by few, yet they are known by their service to God.

For many years I have watched associate pastor Ronnie Guynes at The Potter's House walk in the purpose of serving the people of Africa through MegaCare™. He has worked tirelessly in this calling, as well as made us all aware of how we can lend a hand. The drive and determination he has to build wells, homes, provide food, and educate those who are less fortunate reveals his passion to fulfill the purpose God has for his life.

It is time for you to seize the opportunity to step into your purpose. Grab hold of what God has promised you. You may have to change your surroundings or those surrounding you, but know that it is all worth it.

You must be careful because time and again you will be surrounded by people who do not want you to move forward. They are satisfied with where you are because it makes them comfortable. It is often difficult to let go of people who are close to you. Nonetheless, you must choose whether you want to make them comfortable or make the connection with God.

Often, we allow those who surround us to change our mind from going in the right direction. They continue to speak negativity, which leads to our feelings of guilt for moving forward. This decision will eventually lead us away from our dreams, goals, aspirations, and ultimately, our purpose. I have often seen people who grew up in poor environments become successful, but after a while these same people allow their family and friends who are stuck in the same old place to talk them back into the place they started.

You must hold on to the fact that God chose and predestined you to move into His purpose. You did not create yourself nor did you plan your life. Therefore, it is not your decision or the decision of others to give up on what God ordained you to do.

You cannot become so attached to family, friends, and material goods that you ignore the call of God. Who is holding you back? What are they saying in your ear or around you that will force you to give up on moving into your purpose? What will you miss because you did not change your surroundings or those surrounding you?

It is understandable that you would like those who are surrounding you to be your cheerleaders, but that does not always happen. In fact, after you begin to obey God's voice they may begin to cheer for another team because you have moved out of their comfort zone. Recognize that people come in your life for a reason, season, or a lifetime. Not everyone is meant to walk the entire journey with you. There are some who are only there to give you pearls of wisdom and move on. Then there are those who are to be there as you journey through a particular season in your life. Finally, you have those who will walk with you until the end. Each of those people is important and is a necessity to fulfill the purpose for your life. But you will need to be careful that you do not attach yourself to those who are only there for the reason or season. It is imperative that you look to God because He knows who will be the person for each time. Before you open your heart and expose everything, seek God first. Make sure you are clear in what role this person will play in your life. Proverbs 4:23 (NIV) instructs you to *"guard your heart, for it is the wellspring of life."*

All people are planted in your life for a reason and a set time—even your enemies! Often we look at our enemies as the ones who cause calamity; however, I would suggest to you that these are the ones who help build your faith, trust, and character. At times satan causes conflict to happen between the people we love. Our spouses, children, and friends are often the ones who hurt us the most. It is not detrimental when someone who clearly doesn't like you says something against you. However, if the person you love says something against you, it is often devastating. The choice is in how you will handle the situation. Will you handle it your way or take it to God? God is looking at your reaction.

When someone attempts to convince you that you can't make it, you must find deep in your spirit the determination and perseverance to make it happen. As people attempt to discourage you from achieving your dream, you must find the strength to keep pushing and pursuing. Some of our stumbling blocks are meant to teach us how to jump instead of fall. Our potholes teach us that we may have to take a detour but there is another way around.

God never said achieving His purpose and walking in His way would be easy, but when He chose you He cleared the path. He never made a mistake by choosing you, but you are making the mistake if you are not choosing or following Him. Perhaps you feel that because you are overtaken by drugs, overwhelmed by bills, and overdrawn in your bank account that God did not choose to use you. But I beg to differ. God doesn't call the qualified; He qualifies the called. He does this by allowing us to face many situations and utilizing them as a testimony of His goodness. Stop selling yourself short. You were predestined to fulfill the purpose of God.

Many in biblical times were predestined to serve the purpose of God. And at times they fulfilled their purpose by enduring hardship, pain, and persecution. The Book of Ruth is a clear depiction of someone who was picked out for purpose. Ruth's story is a lesson in how we can turn tragedy to triumph and heartache to hallelujah.

In this story Ruth and Naomi went through the tragedy of losing their husbands. Naomi also lost her sons. After this tragedy, Naomi decided to return to her homeland. Her daughters-in-law, Ruth and Orpah, began the journey with her, to Naomi's dismay. However, Orpah was too connected with the familiarity of her surroundings to continue the journey. Ruth, by contrast, decided she wanted to change. She was ready to change her environment, surroundings, and her God.

> *And Ruth said, Intreat me not to leave thee, or to return from following after thee: for whither thou goest, I will go; and where thou lodgest, I will lodge: thy people shall be my people, and thy God my God: Where thou diest, will I die, and there will I be buried: the Lord do so to me, and more also, if ought but death part thee and me* (Ruth 1:16-17).

Although Naomi had become bitter because of her circumstances, she was still blessed. And because Ruth decided to take hold of the blessing that was on Naomi's life, she too was blessed. Ruth did not see Naomi as Naomi saw herself. Naomi saw herself as bitter and afflicted. However, Ruth saw her as a woman whom she would follow. The tragedy that transpired in Ruth's life was an important part of her achieving the purpose of God. I believe Ruth was blessed *on* purpose *for* purpose.

> *And when she was risen up to glean, Boaz commanded his young men, saying, Let her glean even among the sheaves, and reproach her not: And let fall also some of the handfuls of purpose for her, and leave them, that she may glean them, and rebuke her not* (Ruth 2:15-16).

According to the Scriptures, Boaz commanded his young men to purposefully leave grain for Ruth to glean. Because Ruth made the decision to follow her mother-in-law and believe in her God, Ruth found favor with God and with man. The story continues that Boaz was a kinsman-redeemer and he was able to take Ruth as his wife. Because of this, she became a part of the lineage of Jesus Christ (see Matthew 1). God's purpose for Ruth took her from tragedy to triumph. She was, in turn, blessed on purpose by Boaz because she was predestined for purpose by God.

Naomi's, Ruth's, and Orpah's tragedy is one that I can easily identify with. Even beyond identifying with the death of the spouse, I can also identify with the choice of Ruth and Orpah. I had to choose whether to be as Orpah and surround myself with an environment, people, and things that were familiar, or become like Ruth and change my atmosphere, surroundings, and outlook to walk in my predestined purpose. Although I found it difficult at times to change my surroundings, mentality, and those around me, in retrospect I understand why it was a necessity. There is so much for me to do on this journey. I am filled with God's purpose because He predestined it to be so.

Each of us has been chosen and endowed with the Holy Spirit to live a purpose-filled life. It is not about attaining the material goods or notoriety; it is truly about becoming as a waterfall. You are unselfishly willing to give of yourself to be poured into someone else. God's purpose for your life is intentional and will allow you to see His glory upon your life.

## Chapter 10

# DISFIGURED BUT ANOINTED

*And the vessel that he made of clay was marred in the hand of the potter: so he made it again another vessel, as seemed good to the potter to make it* (Jeremiah 18:4).

*The Spirit of the Lord God is upon me; because the Lord hath anointed me to preach good tidings unto the meek; He hath sent me to bind up the brokenhearted, to proclaim liberty to the captives, and the opening of the prison to them that are bound; to proclaim the acceptable year of the Lord, and the day of vengeance of our God; to comfort all that mourn; to appoint unto them that mourn in Zion, to give unto them beauty for ashes, the oil of joy for mourning, the garment of praise for the spirit of heaviness; that they might be called trees of righteousness, the planting of the Lord, that He might be glorified* (Isaiah 61:1-3).

I didn't know that the pain I felt after the death of my husband would be so excruciating. Neither did I know that the issues, circumstances, and sins I faced would be so difficult to overcome. I've seen my life fluctuate between doing what I know is right and what I know is wrong. Many always say that we just have to live as God has called us to live. And that is true. However, there are some situations that happen in your life that are not easy to conquer.

I am reminded of Second Corinthians 12 where Paul was given a thorn in his flesh. Paul asked that the thorn be removed from his side three times, but God spoke in verse 9 that His grace was enough. It is not always easy to conquer the tragedy, grief, or pain that you endure. There are times when you may feel as though you have reached the point where you can't or won't turn back; however, with one phone call, one circumstance, or one thought you find yourself back in the same place with the same issue. You pray, fast, and read the Word, but the issue, sin, or temptation seemingly intensifies until it overtakes you. The love you feel for God is true, but the issue you are facing in your flesh is so strong that you don't know how to delete it from your thoughts. The anointing and calling on your life is sure, but you are disfigured. The desire in your flesh causes you to become disfigured in the hand of God. Whether it's anger, bitterness, frustration, fornication, adultery, cheating, jealousy, or any other sin or temptation you face, you are now marred in the hand of God.

We are all clay in the hand of the Potter, which is God. We were all anointed and endowed with gifts and talents from God, but many of us don't walk in our gifts because we see the blemishes our issues have caused. The enemy flaunts our weaknesses in our face so often that we become ashamed and refuse to walk in our calling.

Often it is difficult to throw off the sin, temptation, or pain that we endure because it seems to be a part of us. In addition, we suffer through it alone because we feel that we will be judged and branded as unholy. We suffer through it alone because we cannot be transparent with what we actually feel or what we are going through because everyone else appears to be perfect in their holiness. Frequently, we experience the type of issues or situations that we cannot place on the prayer request list or talk about to those who have placed us on the pedestal we never asked to be on. Therefore, we live in this place of disfigurement and loneliness with the hope that one day we will be whole and complete to live the life for Christ.

Bishop T.D. Jakes preached a sermon titled "Alone in the Trial...I Don't Think So!" Bishop Jakes simply stated that "no one teaches you how to suffer." During this sermon, he asked the question of whether you have ever had secret trouble. It is those secret troubles that cause us to feel the loneliness. It's not that you want to be alone, but the trial that you are enduring cannot be communicated to someone else because it is so deep and extremely severe. You feel that you are going through it by yourself. However, the issues you face have been experienced by someone else. The confusion, discontentment, and fear of messing up are being experienced among your family, friends, church members, and even your enemies. People have even reacted to those issues in the same way as you, but the manner in which God will use it to achieve His purpose for you may be different.

Bishop Jakes said, "When God gets ready to use you mightily, He will put you in a predicament where you are alone." That doesn't necessarily mean that you are without people around you, but the feeling that no one can remotely understand is encapsulated in your heart. Your purpose is so important that God allows you to endure the hardships alone because when you don't have the background music from those surrounding you, then you can hear the voice of God more clearly.

When Terry was alive, I sometimes thought my phone would never stop ringing–because we were both always ministering to someone. However, when I began to go through the grief process, the phone stopped ringing. The people God had allowed us to pray for were not calling. Very few people called to pray for me. I was secretly living a life of bitterness and anger because I couldn't tell anyone, and those I wanted to tell were dealing with their own issues. If I had a purpose to fulfill, I was left alone to find it.

It was during these times that I discovered my strengths and weaknesses. I discovered how much I needed God to reign in my life because otherwise I had a one-way ticket to hell. At times I became so inundated with the fact that I was alone, I attempted to do things that would make the loneliness go away. But that didn't work because my loneliness was not meant to satisfy my flesh; it was meant to call to my attention the anointing and purpose God had for my life.

When I endured the tests I often pondered many questions. I wondered how I could be anointed by God and yet not be able to overcome the temptations that I faced. I realized that with every temptation God makes a way of escape, but why didn't I always take that route? How could I know the Word of God and not be able to just stand without falling? Why couldn't I live a holy life without being tormented by the issues of life?

I asked God quite often to take away the pain in my heart, but there were times when it seemed as if God wouldn't answer. What I began to understand was that being shaped into what God had called me to be was a process. It was not a process that would happen overnight, but is in fact a lifelong process. The process is the crushing of your flesh. Just as the olive has to go through the process of pressure to secrete oil, so it is that you must endure the process of pressure to display the anointing of God. God has endowed you with the gifts of the Holy Spirit and set His stamp of approval on you, so you will have the power to walk in authority and fulfill His purpose.

*Now it is God who makes both us and you stand firm in Christ. He anointed us, set His seal of ownership on us, and put His Spirit in our hearts as a deposit, guaranteeing what is to come* (2 Corinthians 1:21-22 NIV).

When a potter takes a lump of clay and places it on the wheel, he doesn't just see the lump of clay; he sees what the desired outcome is beforehand. He also has in mind the intended use of the vessel he has planned to make. However, he understands that before he can see the desired outcome, he must pound the clay to begin its formation. The desire of the potter is not to have a disfigured vessel. Therefore, he is patient with the process of removing all of the huge chunks of clay. He also recognizes that he must be gentle with the clay and utilize another substance to make it soft while shaping and guiding it with his hands. The potter realizes that the process is not finished until the vessel faces and endures the fire. It is while the vessel is in the fire that the impurities from the clay are burned and the shape of the vessel is sealed.

Although the vessel is beautiful, it is not complete. In the final stage of the process, the potter handles the vessel with care and uses his hands to paint the vessel and cover it with beauty. At last the before picture has become a reality, and the vessel is ready for its final destination.

So it is with God and His plan for our lives. He has seen the desired outcome prior to us being formed in the belly and coming out of our mother's womb. He has specifically set us apart for His glory. While we must endure the pounding of sin from our flesh, God is patient with the process. He allows the disfigurement because it is then that we realize how much we need Him. We come to the understanding that we are weak and apt to concede to our sin if we don't have God and His grace in our lives. He utilizes the comfort of the Holy Spirit and His hand to gently guide and shape us into an instrument that He can use. As the potter uses water to achieve uniformity in the clay, God uses His anointing to achieve the uniformity of our calling, gifts, and purpose. The fire of tragedy and challenges removes the impurities of sin in our lives, but it is the Word of God that seals us and makes us beautiful.

When we endure the fiery darts of the enemy, God is there. He knows exactly what needs to be purged and what needs to remain. During the time we are in the fire, God is perfecting the work that He began. He will continue to work on us until the return of Christ. While we walk through life we are steadily becoming the desired picture that God saw beforehand. Once we reach our final destination we too will see the beauty in us that God saw before He formed us.

> *Being confident of this very thing, that He which hath begun a good work in you will perform it until the day of Jesus Christ* (Philippians 1:6).

Your disfigurement was never intended to harm you. The disfigurement actually shows us how much we need God in our life. It is through the tests and trials of life that we find how much we are in need of the Savior to keep us from falling.

> *Now unto Him that is able to keep you from falling, and to present you faultless before the presence of His glory with exceeding joy, To the only wise God our Saviour, be glory and majesty, dominion and power, both now and ever. Amen* (Jude 1:24-25).

## The Blood Covers Our Disfigurement

When I thought of the many adversities I have faced as well as the decisions I made, it was then that God spoke to my spirit. God reminded me that it is the blood of Jesus that covers me. Jesus' blood covered my sins and gave me an opportunity to have a relationship with the Father. It is the blood that can wash away our sins, transgressions, and iniquities. All of our disfigurements, issues, and transgressions are under the blood and should keep us aware that we serve a loving and faithful God. He did not have to sacrifice His Son, but He chose to do it in order to reconcile, redeem, and restore us.

*For it pleased the Father that in Him should all fulness dwell;*
*And, having made peace through the blood of His cross, by Him*
*to reconcile all things unto Himself; by Him, I say, whether they*
*be things in earth, or things in heaven* (Colossians 1:19-20).

God foresaw our lives and all that we would encounter. All of the trials of life teach us that God is always there. He is a very present help in the time of trouble. Anytime we face the concerns and cares of life, God is always there in the fire with us. He doesn't look at what we have done and automatically give up on us. He promised in Hebrews 13:5b, *"I will never leave thee, nor forsake thee."*

We must get to a point where we trust God even when we become disfigured. It is the plan of the enemy to utilize our disfigurement to get us to the point of giving up on worshiping, praising, and talking to God. It is imperative that we remember, even in our weaknesses, that God is our strength. We cannot afford to cut communication with God because it is then that we cut our life support.

I remind you that we are not alone as we experience tumultuous times, but it is God who will walk with us through the entire process. God spoke to us in Proverbs 3:5-6, *"Trust in the Lord with all thine heart; and lean not to thine own understanding. In all thy ways acknowledge Him, and He shall direct thy paths."* If we lean on and acknowledge God for what we need and who He is, we will fulfill the purpose for our life. Our trust in God and knowing that He cannot lie should be the Word that we stand on. Every pain, insecurity, and agonizing moment we experience are the things that God will use to show you who He is to you.

You will begin to recognize Him as Jehovah Jireh (God our Provider), Jehovah Shammah (God our Present Help) and Jehovah Shalom (God our Peace). God has never put a plan into place that was intended to cause you harm, but He will allow the disfigurement so that you will know and understand that He is the only one who will never leave you. You're not alone in the test and trial because God is always there.

> *God is not a man, that He should lie; neither the son of man, that He should repent: hath He said, and shall He not do it? or hath He spoken, and shall He not make it good?* (Numbers 23:19)

> *Trust ye in the Lord for ever: for in the Lord Jehovah is everlasting strength* (Isaiah 26:4).

> *Teaching them to observe all things whatsoever I have commanded you: and, lo, I am with you always, even unto the end of the world. Amen* (Matthew 28:20).

As you endure physical, spiritual, or emotional afflictions, the intensity level for discouragement, depression, lack of trust, or fear is high and at the forefront of your thoughts. I am not an expert on how to act or react to life's challenges, but I know that once we stop for a moment and understand that God is in control and knows our purpose, we will be able to keep moving forward. You will continue to experience the anger, hurt, jealousy, pride, or lack of faith (we all will, we're human), but I encourage you to keep pushing through those emotions. Suicide, homicide, drugs, alcohol, adultery, fornication, and any other impure pursuit is not the way.

Sure, the loneliness is difficult, but this is the time when God invokes His rightful place as Lord and Savior in your life. Get God's Word in your heart and mind. Bring it back to your remembrance. There have been many times when I didn't react in the right manner—at first. But once I stopped throwing the temper tantrum or the pity party, I reminded myself that there is a purpose for my pain that is far greater than what I am enduring.

*And if children, then heirs; heirs of God, and joint-heirs with Christ; if so be that we suffer with Him, that we may be also glorified together. For I reckon that the sufferings of this present time are not worthy to be compared with the glory which shall be revealed in us* (Romans 8:17-18).

*Chapter 11*

# THANK YOU, JESUS!

*Thou art my God, and I will praise Thee:*
*Thou art my God, I will exalt Thee.*
*O give thanks unto the Lord; for He is good:*
*for His mercy endureth for ever* (Psalm 118:28-29).

Recently I have taken a long hard look at the things that have occurred in my life. I've thought about the tragedies, adversities, and sin that have plagued me. I have reflected on the tears I have cried, friends I lost, and the pain I have caused as well as endured. Over the years I have watched others delivered, healed, and saved through the Word God allowed me to preach as I seemingly went in another direction. I have heard sermons that have lifted me from the depths of destruction, only for me to return to the past hurts. I've read God's Word so that I could fight the good fight, keep the faith, and strengthen myself but wasn't able to hold on to what God promised. I also pondered over the times I have allowed anger, bitterness, jealousy, loneliness, frustration, and disobedience to overtake me. I can't count the number of times in my life where it seemed so rough that I wanted to give up. Many moments I lost trust, faith, endurance, and every fruit of the Spirit. I've engaged in sins that were detrimental to the call on my life. And I seemingly reached the point where I felt as if I were too far from God to come back.

So often we get caught in the trap of only looking at the negative aspects of life. Because we have become overwhelmed, worried, and exhausted from the situations that have taken place, we at times forget to accentuate the positive. Many times I have found myself in that place of darkness, but later recognized that there is always light somewhere.

Once in my life I was experiencing a turbulent situation and all I could see was darkness. I felt like I needed to find a hiding place so I literally closed the door and hid myself in a dark room. This is how I measured my life. I couldn't see beyond my situation. As I sat in the dark room, I began to look around. It was quiet and I couldn't see anything but darkness. However, as I looked toward the door, to my surprise there was a glimmer of light. It wasn't much light, but it was enough that I could see it. Through this moment I realized that this light was a symbol of hope. After I saw the light from the door, the revelation hit me. Even though my life was in darkness, it was not the end of the road or my closing moment. It was, in fact, the hope that I needed to at least take another step toward destiny. This pivotal moment showed me that if I focus on the Light of Jesus, there is always light, even in my dark situation. The glimmer of light from the door showed me that God sees something in me that I don't see. He has placed a light in me that will shine through the dark times so that others may see His glory.

*Let your light so shine before men, that they may see your good works, and glorify your Father which is in heaven* (Matthew 5:16).

Think of a situation in your life that could have made a turn for the worse but didn't. Take a moment to think about that one situation, circumstance, or adversity that you thought would push you into losing your mind. Who is the person you lost and thought you couldn't live without? Where is that hole in your heart that you thought could never be mended? How did you survive? What glimmer of hope did you see that kept you from giving up? Have you taken the opportunity to tell God thank you? Countless times you've thought about the difficulties you have faced. But give yourself this time to look back and know God's hand was there and it was all worth it.

You may not be exactly where you want to be or have what you want, but there is hope. Although the light may only be a glimmer, it is still light. We oftentimes want the huge blessings, but we fail to thank God for the little blessings. This is your opportunity to thank God for all of the little blessings you forgot or didn't pay attention to.

I thought I would never see the light through tragedy, but as I focused on each of my situations, I concluded that it could have been worse. I couldn't have written the words in this book if I had not experienced the chaos that life can sometimes bring. There are moments I wanted to run and hide, but God would simply say, "Praise Me, and I will give you the victory."

Psalm 150 gives me the command to praise God, and First Thessalonians 5:18 teaches me to give thanks in everything. I must praise and give thanks in every situation I experience. God is always there, even in the darkest moment. You may have totaled your car in the accident, but you still have your life. You may have buried your spouse, but you were able to experience their unconditional love. You may experience the fiery furnace or the lion's den, but God is always in there with you. Jesus deserves all of our praise and gratitude. He didn't have to do the things He has done for us, but He did. He has never left us. Although we sometimes felt like He left, He was there all of the time. We couldn't survive any part of our life without Him.

It is hard for me to now imagine living my life without Christ. I couldn't walk this journey by myself. For all of that, I must say, "Thank You, Jesus!"

> *Praise Him for His mighty acts: praise Him according to His excellent greatness. Let every thing that hath breath praise the Lord. Praise ye the Lord* (Psalm 150:2,6).

> *In every thing give thanks: for this is the will of God in Christ Jesus concerning you* (1 Thessalonians 5:18).

> *Give thanks unto the Lord, call upon His name, make known His deeds among the people. Sing unto Him, sing psalms unto Him, talk ye of all His wondrous works* (1 Chronicles 16:8-9).

I'm still here! I'm still covered by the blood of Jesus. I have another chance to truly live for God. I have breath in my body and can still utilize all of my limbs. My mouth can still speak. My hands can clap together. I have the ability to think of God's goodness. With all of that being said, I've got to tell Jesus thank you! He has been so awesome to me through the good and bad, ups and downs, as well as right and wrong.

Whenever someone gives you something it is common courtesy to say thank you. Whether they give you a word from God, money, or a smile it's always appropriate to say thank you. So please allow me a moment to thank Jesus for what He has done and who He has been in my life.

Jesus, thank You:

- For every breath You have given me.
- For saving my soul.

- For the death, burial, and resurrection.
- For keeping me when I did not want to be kept.
- For keeping me when I was disobedient and deep in sin.
- For forgiving me, giving me mercy, and loving me through the rough times.
- For Your faithfulness.
- For being my strong tower, refuge, strength, and help in time of trouble.
- For being my Creator, Sustainer, and my Rock.
- For being my peace, love, and joy in times of sorrow.
- For giving me hope to make it another day.
- For my family, friends, church family, and enemies.
- For not giving up on me and letting me go when I deserved it.
- For giving me another chance.
- For chastisement.
- For catching my tears, holding my hand, and guiding me through the dark places.
- For protecting and covering me.
- For fighting for me.
- For lifting my head.
- For not taking Your Holy Spirit away from me.
- For the gifts of the Spirit You have placed inside of me.
- For Your promises.
- For Your intercession on my behalf.
- For giving me life more abundantly.

- For taking me from glory to glory.

- For accepting me as Your own.

- For hearing my prayers.

- For giving me victory.

- For making me more than a conqueror.

- For reviving, renewing, and restoring me.

- For healing me spiritually, mentally, emotionally, and physically.

- For giving me favor with You and with man.

- For allowing me into Your presence.

- For my daughters and the calling on their lives.

- For giving me what I need and even the desires of my heart.

- For being there when I called.

- For answering my questions.

- For carrying me when I was too weak to make the journey.

- For teaching me Your ways.

- For NEVER changing.

- For always being true to Your Word.

- For Your will in my life.

- For ordering my steps and instructing me.

- For Your Holy Word.

- For giving me PURPOSE!

Many times in churches I've heard people say, "Count your blessings and name them one by one." I know this is something that I will never be able to do. What I mean is that I could never count *all* of them. For example, I think about the fact that God has given me breath every day of my life. When I really reflect over the years I've been on earth, I realize that I will never be able to thank God for breath alone. For example, if I took 100 breaths per day for 365 days then I have taken 36,500 breaths per year. If I multiply each breath per year by the number of years I have been living, it would total over 1.5 million breaths! That's a lot of blessing counting, and that number doesn't even include all of the other blessings God has provided for me!

Being thankful is not just something you say, it is something you exemplify. When I worship and praise God I am showing Him how thankful I am. When I take care of my body, mind, and spirit, I am showing God that I am thankful. As I treat people nicely and have the right attitude, it is then that I am showing God my thankfulness.

I realize that God did not have to send His only begotten Son for me so that I could be redeemed, but He did it anyway. It is not often that people will sacrifice something or someone they love for your sake. However, God's love for us is a gift that He offered to us even when we didn't deserve it. I am forever grateful to God for all that He has done in my life.

There have been too many times in my life where I counted myself as unworthy to receive His blessings. However, because God sees beyond my faults, issues, and insecurities I must say thank you for giving me a purpose to fulfill. Even though I wanted to give up on what He ordained me to complete, God kept me safe in His arms. He continued to mold me into what He called me to be.

Although I am not a finished product, I know that I am a work in progress. I know I am thankful to God for not giving up on me even when I gave up on Him. Every morning I awake, I look to God and tell Him thank you. I'm thankful for Him choosing me to be His own. With every fiber of my being I am determined to let God know I have a grateful heart. I am glad that God didn't let me go, but gave me another opportunity to show Him my gratitude.

*Enter into His gates with thanksgiving, and into His courts with praise: be thankful unto Him, and bless His name* (Psalm 100:4).

*My mouth shall speak the praise of the Lord; and let all flesh bless (affectionately and gratefully praise) His holy name forever and ever* (Psalm 145:21 AMP).

Though it is not always easy to quickly see the light in darkness, know that with God the light is always there. Your struggles may be difficult to overcome at this time, but take the time to thank God that your struggles can become your strength. Your pain can become your perseverance and progress. Your obstacles can become your opportunities. Being grateful is a way that you can defeat the fiery darts of the enemy. The enemy yearns to thwart every opportunity for you to see God's goodness and remain faithful to Him. Satan does not try to say that God has not done anything for you, but rather, he attempts to magnify the things you haven't received. However, when you take the opportunity to focus on the things God has done and even what He will do, you will find that God is well deserving of your thankfulness. Don't waste another breath that God has given you on saying words that will please satan, but instead use every breath to bless our Holy God and fulfill the purpose for your life.

*IT IS A GOOD THING TO GIVE THANKS UNTO THE LORD, AND TO SING PRAISES UNTO THY NAME, O MOST HIGH* (Psalm 92:1).

*Chapter 12*

❧

# IT'S NOT OVER!

*My grace is sufficient for thee: for My strength is made perfect in weakness* (2 Corinthians 12:9a).

❧

In December 2007, I was invited to take a seven-day cruise to Grand Cayman, Cozumel, Belize, and Honduras. One of my best friends invited me to spend this time with her and her family. I was elated about this opportunity because I really needed a break from the challenges life can bring. Once I arrived at the port I missed my girls, but there was a feeling of liberty that overwhelmed me. As we boarded the ship and entered our room, I admired and was amazed at the beautiful sight outside my window. I had sailed on other cruises, but never had an opportunity to stay in a room with a balcony. As we pulled from the dock, I sat on the balcony with the wind in my hair and began to think, *This is the life!* As I watched the waves of the water crash against the pier I wondered where I would be if I had given up before now. Would I be enjoying the goodness of the Lord? What other opportunities would I have missed? Amidst the challenges I faced and the numerous times I wanted to quit, I could have missed the beauty that was before me.

We talk a lot about the challenges of life, and though they are tough, what about the joy and happiness of life? This was not only a vacation; it was also a time of reflection of what had taken place in my life.

Have you ever thought that your life was over? Did you feel that because of the decisions you made, sins you committed, or your reaction to challenges that your life would end without fulfilling God's plan and purpose? Do you ask yourself, what is God's plan for your life? How will you overcome the thoughts of giving up? My encouragement to you is that it's not over. Though you may have many questions concerning God's plan, your life is about to begin anew. I understand how we get to the point where we feel that because of the transitions that life can bring, God must've changed His mind. We feel there is nothing that we can offer anyone. However, once God establishes His purpose for your life, He doesn't change His mind.

> *For God's gifts and His call are irrevocable. [He never withdraws them when once they are given, and He does not change His mind about those to whom He gives His grace or to whom He sends His call]* (Romans 11:29 AMP).

I am reminded of the story in Numbers 22 where Balak, the King of Moab, summoned Balaam to curse the children of Israel. However, God instructed Balaam not to curse the people because they were blessed (see Num. 22:12). Although God foreknew the many times the children of Israel would turn their backs on Him, He still called them a blessed people. They were still His chosen people and He never changed His mind. This is the same message to you. Even though satan attempts to curse you, God reminds him that you are blessed.

Do not think for a moment that just because you made some wrong decisions, became angry at your situation, or faced the worst pain of your life that God gave up on you. Your life and all that it encompasses is significant. God will take every obstacle, circumstance, and tragedy we face and turn it into an opportunity to fulfill His purpose.

Many will attempt to curse you through discouragement, things from your past, and sins you have committed. However, God will not allow the curse to prosper in your life. You are still God's beloved.

> *God is not a man, that He should lie, nor a son of man, that He should change His mind. Does He speak and then not act? Does He promise and not fulfill?* (Numbers 23:19 NIV).

After years of grieving I began to think that my life was going no further. I thought I failed God too many times and He was not going to allow me to fulfill His purpose. Thoughts of unworthiness and my inconsistencies caused me to feel far removed from God's presence. I didn't feel I had a purpose anymore. Although I continued to preach God's Word I believed it was only because people knew me, not because God wanted me to minister His Word. I figured God cancelled His purpose for my life.

But as I pondered these thoughts I discovered that I didn't have a clear understanding of the word *purpose*. I have heard the term utilized many times during sermons and also used it when I ministered. But after experiencing many difficulties I had to reevaluate what I thought purpose meant.

Purpose is something you do with intention and determination. It is what you aim to achieve. When we purpose to achieve a goal it simply means that we are determined to reach beyond the difficulties we face and persevere as we continue to move forward. God's purpose for our life was planned intentionally. Every part of our life was ordered by God, but it is up to us to fulfill it. Psalm

37:23-24 states, *"The steps of a good man are ordered by the Lord: and He delighteth in his way."*

I compared the word *ordered* with what we do in a restaurant. As we prepare to dine at a restaurant we are given a menu and the waiter comes to our table to take our order. By then we have scanned the choices on the menu and made our final decision. The waiter usually takes our order in different stages. First, the drink order, appetizer, entrée, and dessert. When ordering our food we have the ability to take out what we don't desire and add what we do desire. We have a choice of when we want which order to come. If we desire to eat the dessert first, then we have that option. The order is then taken to the kitchen staff. They in turn get the necessary ingredients, put them together, and place them in the heat. Once the order is taken, prepared, and returned to us, we then enjoy the end result.

By the same token, God has ordered the steps of our lives. He has set different stages because He knows what we need from the beginning to the end. There are some steps we cannot take as a babe in Christ; therefore, God considers all possible circumstances and consequences before finalizing our steps. He has scanned the menu of our lives and ordered those things that we will need to fulfill His purpose. He carefully identifies what we need and what we will not need to fulfill the calling and purpose for our life. God then prepares us by utilizing the ingredients of faith, salvation, restoration, forgiveness, love, joy, and peace—while at the same time allowing us to be placed in the fire to ensure all of the ingredients are intertwined to achieve the end result. The end result is for us to live life more abundantly in obedience to His will and to have a purpose-filled life.

I also discovered there is a flip side to fulfilling a purpose. There are times when we fail on purpose or intentionally. It is not God's plan for us to fail; however, because we judge ourselves harshly, become overtaken by the burdens of life, and give up because we feel unworthy, we oftentimes sabotage our purpose on purpose. We intentionally ruin our lives by purposefully doing the opposite of what God planned. As I stated previously, often we are engulfed with the fear of failure or fear of success; therefore, we will attempt to disrupt the flow of God.

God has bestowed on us gifts, talents, and anointing. But because we see our failures more than His faithfulness, we become a destructive force in our own lives. We tend to be as the servant who was given one talent and decided to bury it instead of investing it (see Matt. 25:24-27). Many times we take the gift that God has given us, and because we feel unworthy, overwhelmed, or insecure, we will not utilize our gift to fulfill His purpose. It is oftentimes unfortunate that we hide all that God has placed on the inside of us. We must come to the understanding that God doesn't give us that which we do not need. He is well aware of every situation, problem, challenge, issue, and sin that we will face, but has provided the necessities to overcome and be more than conquerors.

Our life is not over until God says that it is over. We must stop attempting to play the god of our lives. Even though we are living this life, we are not in control. Therefore, it is imperative that we don't consider or declare our lives as over just because we experience rough times. Our God is the only one who can take what we consider as a mess and turn it into a wonderful miracle.

When we say it is over, that is when God says it's a new beginning. Your life is not your own because you were bought with a price. If you still have the ability to breathe another moment that means it is not over. As Jesus was on the Cross He stated in John 19:30, *"It is finished."* Then He *"bowed His head and gave up the ghost."* But He was only referring to that particular part. A new beginning started after He stated those words. The beginning of a resurrected life!

If Jesus would have stopped there and thought it was completely over, God's purpose for sending Jesus would not have been completed. You cannot stop because one part of your life is over. Though the divorce is final, the job is lost, or the friends are gone, it is only that part of your life that is over. You must push through the pain of those circumstances to know that this is the beginning of a new chapter. Don't become trapped into thinking that the issue, problem, or hindrance has placed a period at the end of your life. The period is only for that season of your life. A period ends a sentence, yet it still leaves the opportunity to begin a new sentence afterward. Only God determines when the last period will be placed on your life and nothing else comes afterward.

I found that each challenge was the potential for a new beginning as I began to receive an in-depth study of God's Word. I discovered that life was not over because of the obstacles, problems, or the pain, but they were in fact an integral part of working out God's purpose for my life.

I compared my life and all of its challenges with a pregnant woman. When a woman becomes pregnant, fertilization takes place as the sperm and egg connect. Once this connection takes place there are several physical as well as emotional changes that will occur during the term of pregnancy. The woman has to determine in her mind that she will work through these changes and follow the instructions of the doctor. Although the instructions are often quite simple, there are still unexpected obstacles that could be faced during the pregnancy. Many times during the pregnancy a woman feels as though she wants to give up because of the pain and discomfort she experiences. It is during these uncomfortable times that tears are shed and emotions are overwhelming. However, she is determined to endure because her expectation at the end of the pregnancy is to have a baby.

In the same way, God has impregnated us with the Holy Spirit and the seed of His Word. Our spirit has connected with His Spirit. Because of this connection we experience many changes in life. These changes are often more than spiritual. We must be focused and determined to listen to and follow the instructions of God's Word. Although God's Word is not difficult to follow, we will still face many difficulties. During these difficulties we want to give up and quit because the situations and tragedies we face, as well as the sins we commit, are uncomfortable and extremely painful. However, we must be determined to endure the discomfort and pain because of the end result—which is fulfilling the purpose of God and reaching our destiny.

I didn't understand until recently how the pain of losing Terry and experiencing the challenges of life would birth someone else. I was pregnant with purpose and part of this purpose was to give life to another person. Now I began to ask myself how many people God had impregnated me with. The Word and the testimony God has given me are the things that will deliver someone from the clutches of the enemy. It may be that one word or testimony will cause someone to say, *I can't give up because it's no longer an option. It is not my decision or my right to say that my life is over. My life does not belong to me, but to God.* He has entrusted me to live life abundantly so that others may see His goodness and glorify Him. Though the storms have encompassed me and my failures have been many, I am still a yielded vessel to God. While I am yet going through the process, God's purpose for my life is moving toward progress. I know my life is not over because God's purpose for my life has not been completed.

Each day we awake is another opportunity for us to walk in the calling on our life. From the moment I understood God's purpose I was determined to fulfill it. I must fulfill this purpose intentionally and with fortitude in spite of the hindrances I may face. Even though I will oftentimes make the wrong decision or turn down the wrong road that doesn't mean my life is over. For me it means that this is God's opportunity to take this part of my life and show me how to utilize it for His glory.

God's design for my life includes those difficult situations that will push me to reach beyond what I see or feel to achieve His purpose. I want to continue in God's plan for my life. I am willing to suffer through obstacles because I know if I endure there is a crown of glory. Not only do I know there is a crown, but also I know there is a soul waiting to hear my story of God's goodness. There may be so many things that I have yet to experience in this life, but I am going to live each day knowing that God is going to use me in some way. It may not be something so noteworthy that it will make the news, but it may bring a smile to someone's face or help someone fulfill their God-given purpose.

Many times I sit in my office and thank God I didn't give up. I remember looking into the eyes of my daughters and knowing that I do have a purpose. My girls and I have endured some hard times, but that has made each of us stronger in Christ and in our relationship with each other. God's presence in me has allowed me to make a positive presence in their lives. My life is not over because I know there are at least three people in my life that God has given me to help fulfill their purpose.

While writing this book I finally came to the conclusion that the purpose God has for my life included you. Although this book helped me to work through my pain and the thoughts of giving up, it also showed me that you were a part of God's plan for my life. If I had not experienced all of the issues over these years, I would not have the words to write to you. We may never speak face-to-face or share moments of reflection, but through our connection to God we are now brothers and sisters with a God-given purpose.

I have purposed in my heart that no matter how much pain I have to endure, I will keep striving for those who are on the verge of giving up and those who don't have a relationship with God. Although the vicissitudes of life bring more than I can handle, they do not bring more than God can handle. I have learned that as long as God is directing, instructing, correcting, and loving me through life, I will make it. Life will always bring the best and worst of times, but with God it will all work for the good.

Life can be like a relay race. As we run this race we are to hand someone else the baton. Whether it is the baton of faith, courage, strength, or perseverance we should run with someone else on our mind. Do not get caught up in the enemy's trap or idiosyncrasies. The devil is attempting to destroy you because of what is on the inside of you. He is well aware that you are impregnated by God and your purpose is to snatch your loved ones, friends, co-workers, church members, and even your enemy out of hell.

> *But you, beloved, build yourselves up [founded] on your most holy faith [make progress, rise like an edifice higher and higher], praying in the Holy Spirit; guard and keep yourselves in the love of God; expect and patiently wait for the mercy of our Lord Jesus Christ (the Messiah)—[which will bring you] unto life eternal. And refute [so as to] convict some who dispute with you, and on some have mercy who waver and doubt. [Strive to] save others, snatching [them] out of [the] fire; on others take pity [but] with fear, loathing even the garment spotted by the flesh and polluted by their sensuality* (Jude 1:20-23 AMP).

What family member, friend, co-worker, or stranger has God impregnated you with? Do you believe that God can use your issues to help someone else make it through their situation? Take the time to reflect on the people you have helped throughout your life. It doesn't have to be something huge or even something everyone knew you did. It is sometimes little things that God has us do when fulfilling His purpose. Whether you have given clothes and food to a shelter, given help to someone on the corner, helped a child across the street, or visited someone in prison to share God's Word, that is a part of your purpose.

These words are meant to encourage you to continue your life because your purpose includes someone else. You cannot give up because you are also pregnant with purpose. Do not give place to the enemy to abort or miscarry what God has placed on the inside of you. Of course there will be discomfort, changes, and difficult seasons where you want to give up; however, the end result will be one that is pleasing to God.

For many reasons you are still here. You didn't give up when the pain became unbearable. You have stood the test of time. You survived. You have a purpose to fulfill and a destiny to reach. I encourage you to keep the faith and never give in to the pressures of life. Know that God is always with you and has preordained His purpose for your life. You are not alone. He is well aware of every circumstance, issue, tragedy, and sin you will ever face. Yet He loves, cares for, and chose you. Walk in the calling and plan of God every day, and you will get the victory.

*Therefore, since we are surrounded by such a great cloud of witnesses, let us throw off everything that hinders and the sin that so easily entangles, and let us run with perseverance the race marked out for us. Let us fix our eyes on Jesus, the author and perfecter of our faith, who for the joy set before Him endured the cross, scorning its shame, and sat down at the right hand of the throne of God. Consider Him who endured such opposition from sinful men, so that you will not grow weary and lose heart* (Hebrews 12:1-3 NIV).

Revelation 3:20-21 states:

*Behold, I stand at the door, and knock: if any man hear My voice, and open the door, I will come in to him, and will sup with him, and he with Me. To him that overcometh will I grant to sit with Me in My throne, even as I also overcame, and am set down with My Father in His throne.*

If you are reading this book and you do not have a relationship with God, I invite you to do so now. Having an intimate relationship with God is the way for you to survive the pains of life. As you repeat these words, know that God is listening to your voice and looking at your heart. He is ready to accept you in His loving arms.

*Father, in the name of Jesus, I confess that I need You in my life. I believe that You are God and You raised Jesus from the dead. I believe Jesus died, was buried, and rose just for me. Today, I ask You to come into my heart. Live inside of me and show me Your way. Take complete control of my life. Save me from the clutches of the enemy. I believe that I am now Yours. Thank You for giving me life and accepting me as Your own. Amen.*

If you prayed the prayer of salvation, welcome to the Kingdom of God. The angels in Heaven are rejoicing, and so am I! It's time to begin a new journey with a new purpose. Take pleasure in every moment, be thankful at all times, and live life to the fullest. In every moment always remember God is there. Honestly, I cannot tell you that you will not endure any pain, but I do know that you have an intercessor and advocate on your behalf.

Now it's time for you to walk in your purpose and reach your destiny!

*Appendix A*

# My Moments From the Heart

The following are excerpts from my journals, which I have included in order to share with you **my prayers and thoughts to God.**

## *November 6, 2002*

I remember the years that have passed since his death and realize that God alone gave me strength. I am different. I think differently. My reactions are different. I treat my family, friends, and even enemies differently. My motto is: live with no regrets. Now I say *I love you* without hesitation. I make people laugh instead of livid. I am inspired instead of insecure. I am not as sad as I was three years ago. I don't sleep on his side of the bed like I did two years ago. I don't cry as much as I did a year ago. I still remember and miss Terry very much, but now I look at the relationship that has developed between my Creator and me. Of course, there were times that I didn't know whether I still had a relationship with God. I felt like He let me go. I couldn't understand why this tragedy had come upon me. I see couples every day who don't love each other and treat each other like crap. That wasn't my story. I asked myself why this happened to my husband. I couldn't understand what good could possibly come out of this. However, after slowly coming back to God and rebuilding the strong relationship we had before, I came to the conclusion that *my* life wasn't over and *His purpose* for me was just beginning. Do I know exactly what the purpose is…no, but each day I'm sure God will reveal more.

When looking in a mirror, I see more and more of Him in me. November 6, 1999, was a sad day and it broke me down, but it was the brokenness that brought me closer to knowing that God has a purpose planned for my life. Looking in the eyes of my daughters and knowing that I've been given the responsibility to train them in God's way tells me I have a purpose. Talking to other widows and encouraging them to hold on tells me I have a purpose. Preaching and teaching the Word of God shows me that I have a purpose. Do I like the challenges I have faced? Not necessarily. But I know that with every challenge there is Someone who loves me beyond measure and will walk with me every step.

I'm not sure of what I will face tomorrow but I know whatever it is…God is there.

Signed,
*Sharon*

## *July 2004*

As God began to teach me His ways, I had to yield my mind and change my attitude. Yielding my mind and changing my attitude required becoming truthful with myself and owning my actions. Throughout the ordeal my attitude and thinking were plagued with enormous amounts of negative statements to others and myself. My actions and reactions were horrific! I needed to be taught how to speak eloquent words of wisdom to my spirit and about myself. In my mind all that I exemplified during that time was a negative viewpoint; however, the statements God spoke about me were contrary to my words. God said in First Peter 2:9-10 (AMP) concerning me:

*But you are a chosen race, a royal priesthood, a dedicated nation. [God's] own purchased, special people, that you may set forth the wonderful deeds and display the virtues and perfections of Him Who called you out of darkness into His marvelous light. Once you were not a people [at all], but now you are God's people; once you were unpitied, but now you are pitied and have received mercy.*

As Patti LaBelle so eloquently stated, "I got a new attitude!" I have a new attitude because of my life's journey. The journey has been long and tedious yet enlightening. When the journey began I had no expectations but knew the desire of my heart was to please the Lord with my life. The attitude and mindset I had after Terry's transition wasn't who I was or wanted to be. I knew deep inside there was a vibrant and joyful person full of life, but I had to rediscover me and renew my mind. Instead of speaking negatively to and about myself, I came to the realization of what the Word says in Proverbs 18:21, *"Death and life are in the power of the tongue: and they that love it shall eat the fruit thereof."* I was determined not to be the same person and stay in the same predicament. Psalm 40:1-13 (AMP) was one of the Scriptures that helped me to endure:

*I WAITED patiently and expectantly for the Lord; and He in-clined to me and heard my cry. He drew me up out of a horrible pit [a pit of tumult and of destruction], out of the miry clay (froth and slime), and set my feet upon a rock, steadying my steps and establishing my goings. And He has put a new song in my mouth, a song of praise to our God. Many shall see and fear (revere and worship) and put their trust and confident reliance in the Lord. Blessed (happy, fortunate, to be envied) is the man who makes the Lord his refuge and trust, and turns not to the proud or to followers of false gods. Many, O Lord my God, are the wonderful works which You have done, and Your thoughts toward us; no one can compare with You! If I should declare and speak of them, they are too many to be numbered. Sacrifice and offering You do not desire, nor have You delight in them; You have given me the capacity to hear and obey [Your law, a more valuable service than] burnt offerings and sin offerings [which] You do not require. Then said I, Behold, I come; in the volume of the book it is written of me; I delight to do Your will, O my God; yes, Your law is within my heart. I have proclaimed glad tidings of righteousness in the great assembly [tidings of uprightness and right standing with God]. Behold, I have not restrained my lips, as You know, O Lord. I have not concealed Your righteousness within my heart; I have proclaimed Your faithfulness and Your salvation. I have not hid away Your steadfast love and Your truth from the great assembly. Withhold not Your tender mercy from me, O Lord; let Your loving-kindness and Your truth continually preserve me! For innumerable evils have compassed me about; my iniquities have taken such hold on me that I am not able to look up. They are more than the hairs of my head, and my heart has failed me and forsaken me. Be pleased, O Lord, to deliver me; O Lord, make haste to help me!*

No matter how good, bad, or indifferent each season of my life has been, it continues to work together for the good toward the purpose that God has planned for my life. Have I wanted to give up...yes! Do challenges push me to wanting to give up...yes! But will I give up...no! My hope and prayer is what Jesus told Peter in Luke 22:31-32, *"Simon, Simon the enemy comes to sift you as wheat, but I have prayed for you that your faith faileth not and when you are converted strengthen the brethren."* It is a blessing to know that God doesn't sit in judgment of what my flesh does but looks at my heart because I was designed for a purpose.

All I wanted was and is for God to continue loving me in spite of all of my craziness. I know I have faith, and with each test will come more maturity and confidence in who I am in Christ. I will live a Christian life no matter how difficult the road may become. As Psalm 40 says, I delight to do God's will and His Word is in my heart. Although I have failed in some areas, God has never forsaken or given up on me. If God can trust me, then without a shadow of doubt I should trust Him. Thank You, Lord, for everything!

Signed,
*Sharon*

# March 2007

## Pursue and Recover

*And David enquired at the Lord, saying, Shall I pursue after this troop? shall I overtake them? And he answered him, Pursue: for thou shalt surely overtake them, and without fail recover all* (1 Samuel 30:8).

According to *Merriam-Webster's Collegiate Dictionary*, to *pursue* is to "follow in order to overtake." God is giving you the same instruction He gave David...to pursue and recover all! Circumstances have plundered your life of joy, peace, faith, and finances. The plunderer (satan) has attempted to snatch all of your fruit. The enemy's assignment is to kill, steal, and destroy everything inside of you. His fiery darts are worry, fear, doubt, loneliness, illness, lack, and unhappiness to name a few. Everything that you have worked, prayed, and fought to obtain is seemingly taken from you. You may feel as if you are Job and one tragedy after another begins to happen. You've experienced calls from the bill collector, disciplinary actions given to your child from school, unfavorable medical diagnosis, miscommunications between you and your spouse, foreclosure on your home, or something similar, and it makes you ask the question, "Where does it end?" Overwhelming feelings of indecisiveness and anxiety plague your mind so much that tears begin to flow; thoughts of giving up and throwing your hands in the air become the norm. It may seem as if the world and God have turned against you and now you feel like you're to blame! It is difficult to be the leader or head of household because everything falls into your lap and there's no one else to point the finger at if something goes wrong. As I experienced these times, this is when I had to encourage myself, pursue, and recover all that was being attacked and stolen.

Jesus has given us permission to take back what the enemy has stolen. In First Samuel 17, David took back the dignity of Israel by force when he killed Goliath. As David volunteered to take out the Philistine giant, the giant saw David as a little person and thought it was insulting for David to come against him. What the Philistine giant didn't know was that David was not defending Israel alone but came in the name of the God of Israel. Once David pursued the giant in the name of God, the battle was already won. Although David chose five smooth stones, he only needed to use one because God does not need to fight the same battle over and over. He will be victorious the first time and every time. Hebrews 13:8 (NIV) states that *"Jesus Christ is the same yesterday, today and forever."* The giants (circumstances) that we face can be killed; however, they cannot be killed in our own strength. Our strength is not strong enough to overcome and conquer the challenges we face. We do not have the mentality that is necessary to overcome on our own. It is imperative that we hold on to the belief that no matter how bad we may be wounded during battle, with God on our side, the war will be won. We must remember that at the end of everything we win! By submitting to God's voice and guidance, in the name of Jesus we can be more than a conqueror!

*Nay, in all these things we are more than conquerors through Him that loved us* (Romans 8:37).

The enemy looks upon us as being weak with no power to fight. He doesn't recognize the fact that we did not come in our name, but in the name of the Most High God.

*And Moses said unto God, Behold, when I come unto the children of Israel, and shall say unto them, The God of your fathers hath sent me unto you; and they shall say to me, What is His name? what shall I say unto them? And God said unto Moses, I AM THAT I AM: and He said, Thus shalt thou say unto the children of Israel, I AM hath sent me unto you* (Exodus 3:13-14).

When Moses asked the Lord, "What is His name?" God replied to Moses, "I AM THAT I AM sent you." El-Shaddai, meaning God Almighty, has given us the authority to say to our circumstances, "I AM THAT I AM sent me." He has given us power to overcome any situation by speaking the Word. Use it! God has instructed us in Matthew 21:21, *"Jesus answered and said unto them, Verily I say unto you, If ye have faith, and doubt not, ye shall not only do this which is done to the fig tree, but also if ye shall say unto this mountain, Be thou removed, and be thou cast into the sea; it shall be done."* While it seems big, the power in our tongue is more powerful. Proverbs 18:21 says, *"Death and life are in the power of the tongue."*

This mountain of circumstances is but a light affliction. According to God these afflictions are only but for a moment and are temporary.

*For which cause we faint not; but though our outward man perish, yet the inward man is renewed day by day. For our light affliction, which is but for a moment, worketh for us a far more exceeding and eternal weight of glory; While we look not at the things which are seen, but at the things which are not seen: for the things which are seen are temporal; but the things which are not seen are eternal* (2 Corinthians 4:16-18).

It may seem like days, weeks, months, and even years of fighting but to God it is a moment. When the moment ends you'll be victorious.

*Weeping may endure for a night, but joy cometh in the morning* (Psalm 30:5).

As Job endured all of the many tragedies, he declared in Job 23:10, *"But he knoweth the way that I take: when he hath tried me, I shall come forth as gold."* I encourage you to recognize and remember that God already knows the circumstances and issues that you will face. Now I am encouraged!

Signed,
*Sharon*

# *June 2007*

*And I am convinced and sure of this very thing, that He Who began a good work in you will continue until the day of Jesus Christ [right up to the time of His return], developing [that good work] and perfecting and bringing it to full completion in you* (Philippians 1:6 AMP).

I was at the lowest point in my life and I gave up in my heart and mind. The excruciating pain my heart experienced taught me to avoid building a relationship with anyone because at any moment they could leave me, especially through death. I lost all energy to fight the wiles of the devil. I experienced "Footprints in the Sand" because God carried me through the tough times that I deserted Him, feeling as if I was at the end of my rope. Isaiah 26:3 *says, "Thou wilt keep him in perfect peace, whose mind is stayed on Thee: because he trusteth Thee."* Honestly, there were days that I didn't want to be kept, or so I thought. There were tragedies that occurred that seemed as if they were literally trying to take the life out of me. All I knew was that I was grasping for breath and struggling to give voice to what was screaming on the inside of me. Going forward wasn't an option at this time. Living a life once full of purpose, I wanted to become stagnant. To me that meant protection from the possibility of being hurt. It meant that I could shut down and function at my own pace. I know it may sound ludicrous; however, when you experience setback after setback and no victories, you somehow take matters into your own hands and say enough is enough. Realizing that God had been gracious to me, I made a decision to at least put my feet on the ground and take one step forward. There were days that the step was as simple as going into a different room, a step closer to actually walking outside my house to think! Each step became easier, not because there were no issues to deal with, but I wanted to see whether I could survive the next step. It almost became a game of whether I would overcome the situation. It was important for me to keep trying because if I quit, I would never discover what was ahead the following day. I began to rediscover my first love gradually. It was not that my first love (Jesus) left me, it was the fact that I walked away. I thought He would feel the way I felt when my husband died. I really do believe that Jesus felt the same pain I felt, not because I left but because I serve a God who at every moment is fully aware of my infirmities and has experienced them. When Lazarus died, the human side of Jesus wept. He was hurt in the natural but knew in the spiritual that he would soon come back to life (see John 11). These moments for me proved to be what I needed to move to the next level of having more faith in God as well as more faith in the fact that God has a purpose for my life.

Thank You, Jesus!
*Sharon*

# *July 2008*

During this season the economy is taking its toll on our lives. Each day thousands are losing their jobs, pensions, 401(k), savings, homes, cars, hope, faith, and trust. We are facing uncomfortable times more than ever before. It is more than we ever thought we would have to endure. Oftentimes we wonder how we are going to make it through, how we are going to care for our family, and how we are going to survive the storms without losing our minds. My recommendation is to have Jesus in your life. He is the only one that can carry you through every situation. Although you have lost many things, all I can say is that you won't lose the love, faithfulness, mercy, and power of our loving Savior. The material goods can be replaced, but Jesus is irreplaceable. Nothing and no one can ever be all that He is.

I have now been unemployed for a couple of months. At times it is discouraging when I apply for a position and someone else gets it. As I look at my 401(k), IRA, and children's college fund I can't believe how much I have lost. It's hard to see all that you have worked for have a trickledown effect in a manner of months; however, staying focused on the promises of God is all I can do. God has always taken care of us and I don't think He's going to stop now. I must remain faithful to what He has promised.

I don't always understand how I have made it this far, but I know without God I would not have. My financial obligations always outweigh the actual finances I possess, I still face the loneliness, and sin and temptations are always before me, and sometimes I make the wrong decision. However, every month my obligations are met, God comforts me in my lonely times, and there is a word from God that sustains and forgives. God remains faithful and continues to open doors. I have no idea of what tomorrow may bring, but I do know the One who created tomorrow and I trust Him. I can't and don't want to give up because it's not over. I have so much more inside of me to give birth to. I am to give Him glory, honor, and praise daily. That is what I intend to do for the rest of my life even in the midst of my pain. Because it is in the pain that God reveals Himself to me and reassures me that giving up during these times should not be an option.

Thank You, Jesus, for all You have done for me!

Signed,
*Sharon*

*Appendix B*

❦

# "It's Not Over, It's Just Begun!"
# Elder Sharon Grant

**[This is a reprint of an online article written by Nichelle Early, CEO and Executive Editor of PreachingWoman.com]**

Has life ever confronted you with challenges that made you wonder how you would have the strength to live another moment? Have you ever experienced a pressure so great that you've felt like you've missed the mark and it's all over? At one time or another, we've all had those feelings. However, the question is, "How do you navigate the emotional pitfalls of the enemy and recognize that truly, "it's not over?" Well, we have been favored with the exclusive opportunity to talk one on one with Elder Sharon Grant of the world-renowned church, *The Potter's House*, Dallas, TX. She gallantly agreed to be featured on our site and encourage us that, "It's Not Over, It's Just Begun!"

Demonstrating a gentleness and grace matchless by many, Elder Sharon Grant overwhelmingly exudes the dynamic strength of God. Adorned with an uncanny confidence and an awe-striking anointing that is unmistakably birthed from the depths of the presence of God, Elder Grant is on a mission to reach those who are broken-hearted, despondent, and perplexed, and usher them out of the desolate places into an abundant life in the Lord Jesus

Christ. However, Elder Grant will be the first to tell you that this mandate is not without indelible personal experiences that have paradoxically broken and mended her own heart to equip her for the undeniable, relentless call of God upon her life.

August, 1997, Elder Grant publicly acknowledged her call to the ministry. We asked Elder Grant to share with us what that step was like, and here's what she explained:

"That was a 'scary moment,' if you will…because I'm one that cannot handle thinking that I've hurt God. So, I was very intentional about making sure that I heard from him. And through prayer and confirmation by way of a prophetic word…I said yes!"

However, a few years after saying "yes," on November 6, 1999, Elder Grant would experience a personal circumstance that would change her life forever. The Lord expeditiously called her husband, the late Rev. Terry Grant, home to glory. Life as she knew it would end. In her mind, *"it was over."* We asked Elder Grant to speak to us regarding how to navigate through life's darkest moments, without losing heart, and she candidly offered this response:

"In order to be who God has called you to be, you must be broken…The death of my husband facilitated my transition of brokenness before the Lord…I can remember, in January 2003, hearing my pastor, Bishop Jakes, preach a message called *Breaking Point*…I truly felt like I was at my breaking point. But, [over time], I began to see that God changed my life for the good through this most heart-wrenching experience…because it is through this experience that I am able to minister to the broken-hearted and to those who have lost sight of their purpose, " said Elder Grant.

So, we asked Elder Grant, "What advice do you have to offer to women in ministry who may have gone through a similar circumstance as yours, or who are experiencing a broken heart due to personal loss and circumstances?"

"Have your moment...but keep thinking of the goodness of Jesus. Continue to hold on to what God has promised you no matter what. And most importantly, when thou are converted, strengthen your brother, and remember, it's not over!" she said firmly. Elder Grant additionally offered these points of interest:

1. Read the Word of God—"the Word of God gives you the breath to live another moment."

2. Remember, God is the keeper of your soul.

3. Know with assurance that God has not gone anywhere—God is with you in your darkest moment.

4. Consider that God knows the plans He has for you!

5. Remember, "it's not over, it's just begun," encouraged Elder Grant.

Hailing from Atlanta, Georgia, ministry has been an engrafted part of Elder Grant's life from the very beginning. Reared under the watchful eye of loving parents, Pastor and First Lady Thomas Ashford, of the New Jerusalem Missionary Baptist Church, as a "pastor's kid (PK)," Elder Grant observed firsthand the enormous demand that ministry places on your personal life, so she's no stranger to the hard work and perseverance that is necessary to be effective in ministry. She memorably recalls how her parents made great sacrifices for the sake of the work of the Lord—visiting hospitals, praying for the sick, and ministering to the poor and brokenhearted amidst numerous other obligations. At that time, she did not figure that she would also be called to such a life of ministry and servanthood, especially to those that feel bewildered and forsaken. However, God did.

As we understand the challenges that many pastor's kids face, especially upon their decision to accept the call of God, we asked Elder Grant to talk to us from the perspective of being a "PK" embarking upon personal ministry and provide us with some essential principles of doing so and here is what she had to say:

"First, I must say that I have the greatest parents! And, being a pastor's kid entering the ministry afforded me the covering of being protected as a minister, and as a biological daughter, which is very special...and if I could offer three principles, in particular for those that were raised as pastor's kids, and now embarking upon their own personal ministry, I would say:

1. Learn from those who have walked before you—always listen to wise counsel, this will help you avoid a lot of hard places.

2. Guard your heart—sometimes people will attempt to attach themselves to you because of the call of your parents, status, and other motives. And often times this can be hurtful, but you must keep a pure heart.

3. Be who you are—you do not have to imitate anyone else. God created you to be unique. You are peculiar and that makes you special."

# About the Author

Sharon L. Grant is a native of Atlanta, Georgia. She is an ordained elder at The Potter's House, in Dallas, Texas, under the leadership of Bishop T.D. Jakes.

Sharon L. Grant, a preacher, teacher, author, and woman of compassion, has poured herself into helping people spiritually, emotionally, and physically. Her message is filled with inspiration, encouragement, and the boldness of God's Word. Sharon speaks and exemplifies her love and reverence for Jesus Christ through ministering at retreats, conferences, and youth events. She has been featured on PreachingWoman.com in an article entitled "It's Not Over, It's Just Begun!"

Sharon resides in Dallas, Texas, with her three daughters.

For more information or to schedule speaking engagements:

**Sharon L. Grant Ministries**
1301 East Debbie Lane
Suite 102, #323
Mansfield, Texas 76063

www.slgrantministries.com

info@slgrantministries.com

www.myspace.com/sharonlgrant

www.facebook.com/sharon.l.grant

# Key Topic

Page 38
Running low on Spiritual feul

Pg 69 + 74 + 81 (cross)
Preserverance, expectation + patience

Pg 71
Omnipotent - (all powerful)
Ominiscent - all knowing
Ominipresent - ever prensent

Pg 81
4 points (to be able to Triumph in our
own Situations

Pg 79 - Breaking Point
Denied Christ

Pg 88 - commitment to God

Pg 116 - but God.
PAIN, Peace, progress

Pg 141 Being thankful
Showing God.

Pg 145 - purpose

Additional copies of this book and other book titles from DESTINY IMAGE are available at your local bookstore.

Call toll-free: 1-800-722-6774.

Send a request for a catalog to:

## Destiny Image® Publishers, Inc.

P.O. Box 310
Shippensburg, PA 17257-0310

*"Speaking to the Purposes of God for This Generation and for the Generations to Come."*

**For a complete list of our titles,
visit us at www.destinyimage.com.**